VOLUME 7

OLD TESTAMEN

THE NEW COLLEGEVILLE BIBLE COMMENTARY

JOSHUA, JUDGES

Roland J. Faley, T.O.R.

SERIES EDITOR

Daniel Durken, O.S.B.

LITURGICAL PRESS

Collegeville, Minnesota

www.litpress.org

Nihil Obstat: Reverend Robert Harren, *Censor deputatus*.
Imprimatur: ✠ Most Reverend John F. Kinney, J.C.D., D.D., Bishop of St. Cloud, Minnesota, August 30, 2011.

Design by Ann Blattner.

Cover illustration: *Joshua Anthology* by Donald Jackson. Copyright 2010 *The Saint John's Bible*, Order of Saint Benedict, Collegeville, Minnesota USA. Used by permission. Scripture quotations are from the New Revised Standard Version of the Bible, Catholic Edition, copyright 1989, 1993 National Council of the Churches of Christ in the United States of America. Used by permission. All rights reserved.

Photos: pages 14, 33, 110, Wikimedia Commons; pages 21, 76, 107, Photos.com.

Map created by Robert Cronan of Lucidity Information Design, LLC.

Scripture texts in this work are taken from the *New American Bible, revised edition* © 2010, 1991, 1986, 1970 Confraternity of Christian Doctrine, Inc., Washington, DC. All Rights Reserved. No part of this work may be reproduced or transmitted in any form or by any means, electronic or mechanical, including photocopying, recording, or by any information storage and retrieval system, without permission in writing from the copyright owner.

1	2	3	4	5	6	7	8	9

Library of Congress Cataloging-in-Publication Data

Faley, Roland J. (Roland James), 1930–
    Joshua ; Judges / Roland J. Faley.
        p. cm. — (New Collegeville Bible commentary. Old Testament ; v. 7)
    ISBN 978-0-8146-2841-6
    1. Bible. O.T. Joshua—Commentaries.   2. Bible. O.T. Judges—Commentaries.   I. Title.
    BS1295.53.F35   2011
    222'.2077—dc23   2011032231

CONTENTS

ABBREVIATIONS

Books of the Bible

Acts—Acts of the Apostles
Amos—Amos
Bar—Baruch
1 Chr—1 Chronicles
2 Chr—2 Chronicles
Col—Colossians
1 Cor—1 Corinthians
2 Cor—2 Corinthians
Dan—Daniel
Deut—Deuteronomy
Eccl (or Qoh)—Ecclesiastes
Eph—Ephesians
Esth—Esther
Exod—Exodus
Ezek—Ezekiel
Ezra—Ezra
Gal—Galatians
Gen—Genesis
Hab—Habakkuk
Hag—Haggai
Heb—Hebrews
Hos—Hosea
Isa—Isaiah
Jas—James
Jdt—Judith
Jer—Jeremiah
Job—Job
Joel—Joel
John—John
1 John—1 John
2 John—2 John
3 John—3 John
Jonah—Jonah
Josh—Joshua
Jude—Jude
Judg—Judges
1 Kgs—1 Kings

2 Kgs—2 Kings
Lam—Lamentations
Lev—Leviticus
Luke—Luke
1 Macc—1 Maccabees
2 Macc—2 Maccabees
Mal—Malachi
Mark—Mark
Matt—Matthew
Mic—Micah
Nah—Nahum
Neh—Nehemiah
Num—Numbers
Obad—Obadiah
1 Pet—1 Peter
2 Pet—2 Peter
Phil—Philippians
Phlm—Philemon
Prov—Proverbs
Ps(s)—Psalms
Rev—Revelation
Rom—Romans
Ruth—Ruth
1 Sam—1 Samuel
2 Sam—2 Samuel
Sir—Sirach
Song—Song of Songs
1 Thess—1 Thessalonians
2 Thess—2 Thessalonians
1 Tim—1 Timothy
2 Tim—2 Timothy
Titus—Titus
Tob—Tobit
Wis—Wisdom
Zech—Zechariah
Zeph—Zephaniah

The Book of Joshua

The book takes its name from its central character, Joshua, son of Nun, the faithful aide of Moses. He is the designated leader of the Hebrew people as they take possession of Canaan, the Promised Land. In him the leadership of Moses finds its continuation, even to the point of echoing moments of the Mosaic exodus, the crossing of the Jordan (Red Sea) (chs. 3–4) and the renewal of the covenant at Shechem (Sinai) (ch. 24).

In the figure of Joshua, the author(s) of the book continues the early history of Israel, recounting the fulfillment of the promise of land possession, a promise which stands at the heart of the Deuteronomistic history.

The Deuteronomistic History

Although complete in itself, the book of Joshua is actually part of a much longer historical record which proceeds from a particular school of religious thought. As is commonly held today, the book of Deuteronomy served as the inspiration for the historical books which follow it, viz., Joshua, Judges, 1–2 Samuel, and 1–2 Kings. It is the theological perspective of that fifth book of Torah which colors the entire history of Israel from the occupation to the time of the Babylonian exile. That viewpoint can be summarized in the oft-repeated admonition: Fidelity to the Lord's commands brings success, while infidelity brings only failure and rejection (Deut 5:32; 6:24f; 7:4). It is against this background that the dominantly successful career of Joshua is judged.

The record of this history was long in the making, extending over six centuries and comprised of various documents and sources (not all of them in total agreement). If any moment was central in this process, it would have to be the reign of King Josiah (620–609 B.C.) who inaugurated a reform strongly influenced by the thinking of Deuteronomy. In fact, the discovery of a lost book of laws at the time of Josiah's temple renovations (2 Kings 22) is often identified by scholars as an early copy of Deuteronomy. Whatever the evolution of this historical corpus may have been, the final result is clear enough. The accounts of the Israelite monarchy and its precedents, extending back to the twelfth century B.C., provided the Deuteronomists with a framework in which to explain the country's successes and failures from a distinctly theological point of view. If the Assyrians were to destroy the Northern Kingdom of Israel in the eighth century B.C. and Babylon were to do the same in the sixth, the reason was not military or political inferiority but the failure of the Israelites to live as a sacred, covenanted people.

The final editing of the Deuteronomistic History, which included Joshua, comes from a period shortly after the destruction of Jerusalem in 587–586 B.C.

The theology of Joshua

It is the religious perspective on Israel's successes and failures that permeates the book of Joshua. If the occupation of Canaan was marked by success in the invaders' military undertakings, this was simply due to their obedience to the Lord's directives.

The book of Joshua brings to fulfillment the promise initially made to Abraham. That promise was twofold: many descendants and the making of a great nation (Gen 12:2ff). It is with the last part of that promise that this book primarily deals, i.e., the occupation of Canaan, the land of promise.

Covenant fidelity, so important to the Deuteronomist, is centered principally in this book on the first precept of the Decalogue, i.e., the exclusion of false deities. Canaan was a land wherein foreign cult abounded, especially the worship of fertility gods. It is clear throughout that the Hebrews are to see any form of religious compromise as categorically excluded. To underscore the exclusivity of YHWH's sovereignty the book ends with a ceremony of covenant renewal.

The book's division

There are two main sections of Joshua, the first dealing with the occupation of the land of Canaan (chs. 1–12), and the second with the distribution of the land to the twelve tribes (chs. 13–21). The final chapters deal with a dispute regarding a Transjordanian altar (ch. 22), the renewal of the covenant, and the death of Joshua (chs. 23–24). The account of the occupation does not extend to the entire territory which later made up the country but is more limited and centered around the land of the tribe of Benjamin. The documentation underlying this narrative of seizure is considered very ancient, probably dating from the twelfth century, whereas the text dealing with land distribution dates from the time of the established monarchy.

Joshua and history

When it comes to a historical appraisal of the Joshua narrative, the reader must proceed with a measure of caution. The book forms part of the "historical" literature primarily because it is a broad record of the country's origins and early development. That is not to make of it a totally objective picture of what actually transpired, refraining for the moment from the question of whether historical accounts are ever objective. The book, for example, presents the occupation of Canaan in lightning fashion, with little or no strong military opposition. That the actual occupation was a much slower process of elimination and incorporation is evident from both biblical (see Judg 1–3) and extra-biblical sources. The destruction of Jericho and Ai is evidently more idealistic than real, with archeological evidence pointing to no significant occupation of those cities during the period of the Israelite incursion. As we shall see, there are other instances of difficulty in squaring the biblical data with other historical sources. What is intractable, however, is the appearance of the Hebrews in Palestine in the twelfth century B.C.

All of this is but to say that a theological perspective is dominant in this and the other historical books of the Old Testament. The land was a gift of the covenant God to the Israelite population and, regardless of the actual circumstances that made this a reality, the basic belief is never compromised. This accounts for the marked idealization which is present in the story of the occupation.

The figure of Joshua

While Joshua was certainly a towering figure at the time of the conquest, historical accuracy does not permit us to see him as responsible for all the remarkable strides taken in the book that bears his name. He is presented as the idealized hero of the conquest and the one who presided over the subsequent distribution of the land. But the fact is that much of the activity presented in the first twelve chapters is localized, largely related to the single tribe of Benjamin and its sanctuary at Gilgal. The land of Canaan was brought under control only after a century of Israelite expansion, and the account of the allotment of the land largely reflects the period of the monarchy.

Yet in all of this Joshua stands as a larger than life figure. Not unlike Moses, he has been drawn to some events recorded in this book more in spirit than in fact. It is under the mantle of his leadership that the events of the occupation of the land find their appropriate setting.

The Book of Joshua

I. Conquest of Canaan

1 **Divine Promise of Assistance.** ¹After Moses, the servant of the LORD, had died, the LORD said to Moses' aide Joshua, son of Nun: ²Moses my servant is dead. So now, you and the whole people with you, prepare to cross the Jordan to the land that I will give the Israelites. ³Every place where you set foot I have given you, as I promised Moses. ⁴All the land of the Hittites, from the wilderness and the Lebanon east to the great river Euphrates and west to the Great Sea, will be your territory. ⁵No one can withstand you as long as you live. As I was with Moses, I will be with you: I will not leave you nor forsake you. ⁶Be strong and steadfast, so that you may give this people possession of the land I swore to their ancestors that I would give them. ⁷Only be strong and steadfast,

---

POSSESSION OF THE LAND

Joshua 1–12

1:1-18 Preparatory injunctions

The chapter is clearly Deuteronomistic in character and style: YHWH's assurance of success in return for law observance (1:1-9); Joshua's injunction to prepare for the conquest (1:10-11); and the admonition to the three Transjordanian tribes to participate in the military action (1:12-18).

In the promise of divine protection and the injunction to fidelity (1:3-7. cf. Deut 30:15-20), there are elements of both the real (v. 3) and the ideal (v. 4), with the latter granting borders extending from the Mediterranean in the west to the Euphrates in the east. The law to be strictly observed (1:7-8) is that enunciated by Moses after the battle of Sihon and Og (Deut 1:3-5) and later in its written form to be read in assembly every seven years (Deut 31:9-11). It is the book of Deuteronomy which is intended.

▶ This symbol indicates a cross-reference number in the *Catechism of the Catholic Church.* See page 124 for number citations.

being careful to observe the entire law which Moses my servant enjoined on you. Do not swerve from it either to the right or to the left, that you may succeed wherever you go. ⁸Do not let this book of the law depart from your lips. Recite it by day and by night, that you may carefully observe all that is written in it; then you will attain your goal; then you will succeed. ⁹I command you: be strong and steadfast! Do not fear nor be dismayed, for the LORD, your God, is with you wherever you go.

¹⁰So Joshua commanded the officers of the people: ¹¹"Go through the camp and command the people, 'Prepare your provisions, for three days from now you shall cross the Jordan here, to march in and possess the land the LORD, your God, is giving as your possession.'"

The Transjordan Tribes. ¹²Joshua addressed the Reubenites, the Gadites, and the half-tribe of Manasseh: ¹³"Remember what Moses, the servant of the LORD, commanded you when he said, 'The LORD, your God, is about to give you rest; he will give you this land.' ¹⁴Your wives, your children, and your livestock may remain in the land Moses gave you here beyond the Jordan. But all the warriors among you must cross over armed, ahead of your kindred, and you must help them ¹⁵until the LORD has settled your kindred, and they like you possess the land the LORD, your God, is giving them. Afterward you may return and possess your own land, which Moses, the servant of the LORD, has given you east of the Jordan." ¹⁶They answered Joshua, "We will do all you have commanded us, and we will go wherever you send us. ¹⁷As completely as we obeyed Moses, we will obey you. Only, may the LORD, your God, be with you as God was with Moses. ¹⁸Anyone who rebels against your orders and does not obey all your commands shall be put to death. Only be strong and steadfast."

Joshua allows three days of preparation prior to the Jordan crossing from the east, the locale of Moses' death at Nebo at the conclusion of Deuteronomy (1:10-11). The injunction to the three tribes—Reuben, Gad, and one half of Manasseh—is based on an important historical antecedent (1:12-18). These tribes settled in Transjordan and never occupied "the land of Canaan" properly so called (Deut 3:12-20). However, their legitimate status as part of Israel is repeatedly brought to the fore in underscoring the part they played in the occupation. They were not excused from military duty in bringing the Canaanites into subjection. In their submissive response to Joshua's exhortation (1:16-18), they echo the customary response of the covenanted people.

2:1-24 Rahab and the spies

The heroic action of the harlot Rahab wins her recognition in both Testaments (cf. Heb 11:31; Jas 2:25) and finds her a place in the genealogy of Jesus (Matt 1:5).

2 **Spies Saved by Rahab.** [1]Then Joshua, son of Nun, secretly sent out two spies from Shittim, saying, "Go, reconnoiter the land and Jericho." When the two reached Jericho, they went into the house of a prostitute named Rahab, where they lodged. [2]But a report was brought to the king of Jericho: "Some men came here last night, Israelites, to spy out the land." [3]So the king of Jericho sent Rahab the order, "Bring out the men who have come to you and entered your house, for they have come to spy out the entire land." [4]The woman had taken the two men and hidden them, so she said, "True, the men you speak of came to me, but I did not know where they came from. [5]At dark, when it was time to close the gate, they left, and I do not know where they went. You will have to pursue them quickly to overtake them." [6]Now, she had led them to the roof, and hidden them among her stalks of flax spread out there. [7]But the pursuers set out along the way to the fords of the Jordan. As soon as they had left to pursue them, the gate was shut.

[8]Before the spies lay down, Rahab went up to them on the roof [9]and said: "I know that the LORD has given you the land, that a dread of you has come upon us, and that all the inhabitants of the land tremble with fear because of you. [10]For we have heard how the LORD dried up the waters of the Red Sea before you when you came out of Egypt, and what you did to Sihon and Og, the two kings of the Amorites beyond the Jordan, whom you destroyed under the ban. [11]We heard, and our hearts melted within us; everyone is utterly dispirited because of you, since the LORD, your God, is God in heaven above and on earth below. [12]Now then, swear to me by the LORD that, since I am showing kindness to you, you in turn will show kindness to my family. Give me a reliable sign [13]that you will allow my father and mother, brothers and sisters, and my whole family to live, and that you will deliver us from death." [14]"We pledge our lives for yours," they answered her. "If you do not betray our mission, we will be faithful in showing kindness to you when the LORD gives us the land."

[15]Then she let them down through the window with a rope; for she lived in a house built into the city wall. [16]"Go up into the hill country," she said, "that your pursuers may not come upon you. Hide there for three days, until they return; then you may go on your way." [17]They answered her, "We are free of this oath that you made us take, unless, [18]when we

---

The account, which has experienced a process of editorial redaction, revolves entirely around the person of Rahab, the only person identified by name. Its present location argues for its independent origin, now located somewhat artificially between the preparations for occupation (ch. 1) and its beginning (ch. 3). Joshua's spies are sent to reconnoiter the enemy terrain. In the course of the actual battle, all enemy forces, military or civilian, were to be destroyed. The present narrative explains why one family, "the house of Rahab," was ultimately saved. This may well be the original reason for its preservation.

come into the land, you tie this scarlet cord in the window through which you are letting us down. Gather your father and mother, your brothers, and all your family into your house. ¹⁹Should any of them pass outside the doors of your house, their blood will be on their own heads, and we will be guiltless. But if anyone in your house is harmed, their blood will be on our heads. ²⁰If, however, you betray our mission, we will be free of the oath you have made us take." ²¹"Let it be as you say," she replied, and sent them away. When they were gone, she tied the scarlet cord in the window.

²²They went up into the hill country, where they stayed three days until their pursuers, who had sought them all along the road without finding them, returned. ²³Then the two came back down from the hills, crossed the Jordan to Joshua, son of Nun, and told him all that had happened to them. ²⁴They assured Joshua, "The LORD has given all this land into our power; indeed, all the inhabitants of the land tremble with fear because of us."

In addition, it represents the conflict between two forces: the pagan king of Jericho and the faith-filled Hebrews under Joshua. These two forces converge dramatically around the person of Rahab, who handles both with consummate cunning. She deceives the king's emissaries in the matter of the spies' whereabouts and sends them on a vain pursuit (2:3-5). She protects the Israelite spies by hiding them in the flax stalks drying on her roof prior to their being made into linen (2:6). She wrests from them assurance of future protection for herself and her family (2:13-14). Her plan succeeds and the spies are saved. The conflict between the two forces of the chapter clearly points to success for the invaders and destruction for the inhabitants.

Finally, the story is cast in a faith-filled mold, reflecting the final stage of its composition. Rahab recognizes the God of the Hebrews (2:9) and recalls his saving action in the exodus (2:10). It is in recognition of YHWH's power and might that she asks for her own deliverance (2:11-12). The departing spies agree to her request but, in Deuteronomistic form, with certain conditions. The scarlet cord is to be exposed and none of her relatives are to leave the house (2:18-19). The experience shores up the confidence of the spies, who in returning to Joshua assure him of success (2:22-24).

3:1–4:24 The crossing of the Jordan

The crossing begins at Shittim (3:1) or Abel-shittim (Num 33:49), east of the Jordan, and concludes at Gilgal, later an important cultic site, east of Jericho. What is presented is primarily a liturgical procession, situating the historical event in what later became a cultic celebration of the crossing. The underlying sources of the narrative are complex and intertwined although the story line itself remains clear enough. In various ways it is a theological duplicate of the Exodus-Sinai experience.

3 **Preparations for Crossing the Jordan.** ¹Early the next morning, Joshua and all the Israelites moved from Shittim and came to the Jordan, where they stayed before crossing over. ²Three days later the officers went through the camp ³and issued these commands to the people: "When you see the ark of the covenant of the LORD, your God, which the levitical priests will carry, you must break camp and follow it, ⁴that you may know the way to take, for you have not gone over this road before. But let there be a space of two thousand cubits between you and the ark: do not come nearer to it." ⁵Joshua also said to the people, "Sanctify yourselves, for tomorrow the LORD will perform wonders among you." ⁶And he told the priests, "Take up the ark of the covenant and cross ahead of the people"; so they took up the ark of the covenant and went before the people.

⁷Then the LORD said to Joshua: Today I will begin to exalt you in the sight of all Israel, that they may know that, as I was with Moses, so I will be with you. ⁸Now command the priests carrying the ark of the covenant, "When you come to the edge of the waters of the Jordan, there take your stand."

⁹So Joshua said to the Israelites, "Come here and listen to the words of the LORD, your God." ¹⁰He continued: "By this you will know that there is a living God in your midst: he will certainly dispossess before you the Canaanites, Hittites, Hivites, Perizzites, Girgashites, Amorites, and Jebusites. ¹¹The ark of the covenant of the Lord of the whole earth will cross the Jordan before you. ¹²Now choose twelve men, one from each of the tribes of Israel. ¹³When the soles of the feet of the priests carrying the ark of the LORD, the Lord of the whole earth, touch the waters of the Jordan, it will cease to flow; the water flowing down from upstream will halt in a single heap."

The Crossing Begun. ¹⁴The people set out from their tents to cross the Jordan, with the priests carrying the ark of the covenant ahead of them. ¹⁵When those bearing the ark came to the Jordan and the feet of the priests bearing the ark were immersed in the waters of the Jordan—which overflows all its banks during the entire season of the harvest— ¹⁶the waters flowing from upstream halted,

3:1-17 Preparation and crossing

The pre-crossing injunctions are Deuteronomistic in character. The order for the people to "sanctify" themselves involved ritual washing and even abstinence from sexual intercourse (3:2-5; Exod 19:10-14). The ark of the covenant, the throne or footstool of the invisible YHWH also contained the tablets of the law. A reverent distance separated the ark from the people, excluding any physical contact (Exod 19:12; 2 Sam 6:6-7). The role of Levitical priests as ark-bearers at this early stage may be later editorializing, in substitution for the twelve men who were originally designated (3:12). The combination of different sources makes it difficult to distinguish between the role of the priests and the twelve laymen.

standing up in a single heap for a very great distance indeed, from Adam, a city in the direction of Zarethan; those flowing downstream toward the Salt Sea of the Arabah disappeared entirely. Thus the people crossed over opposite Jericho. [17]The priests carrying the ark of the covenant of the LORD stood on dry ground in the Jordan riverbed while all Israel crossed on dry ground, until the whole nation had completed the crossing of the Jordan.

4 Memorial Stones. [1]After the entire nation had completed the crossing of the Jordan, [2]the LORD said to Joshua: Choose twelve men from the people, one from each tribe, [3]and command them, "Take up twelve stones from this spot in the Jordan riverbed where the priests have been standing. Carry them over with you, and place them where you are to stay tonight."

[4]Summoning the twelve men he had selected from among the Israelites, one

---

The occupation is to bring to Joshua the type of recognition reserved for Moses, the original deliverer of God's people (3:6-7; 4:14). The presence of the ark highlights the intervention of YHWH. As the priests reach the river's edge, the waters recede and dry land appears (3:13). An interesting sidelight is the mention of various peoples that occupied Canaan at the time, pointing to the fact that it was not only native Canaanites who were dispossessed (3:10). In fact, the term Canaanite was frequently used for the various ethnic groups occupying the country. In this listing the Hittites were a non-Semitic people known in the south from the time of Abraham (Gen 23:10). The Amorites were well known from pre-Israelite times. The Jebusites occupied Jerusalem. The Hivites are sometimes identified with the known Hurrians, and the Perizzites and Girgasites, generally unidentified.

The crossing takes place at the time of the spring harvest (3:15), coinciding with the time of Passover (5:10). It was a season when the Jordan was swollen from spring rains and the melting snow of Mt. Hermon. The passage of the people is facilitated as the priests and the ark remain motionless in the bed of the river (3:10-13). The account is evocative of Israel's earlier passing through the Red Sea (Exod 14).

4:1-24 The remembrance

Etiology—a way of explaining the causes or origins of something that occurs later—is central to any understanding of much of Old Testament narrative. This is a linkage between memorials or important sites and historical events in the life of the people. The site then served to evoke the memory. The collection of stones from the Jordan, linked with the Gilgal sanctuary, so important to the Benjaminite tradition, became a concrete reminder of the Jordan crossing. It is also a refrain from the Exodus-Sinai experience when twelve pillars were erected to commemorate the covenant with the twelve

15

"The people came up from the Jordan on the tenth day of the first month . . ." (Josh 4:19). The Jordan River defines the borders between Israel and Jordan.

from each tribe, [5]Joshua said to them: "Go to the Jordan riverbed in front of the ark of the LORD, your God; lift to your shoulders one stone apiece, so that they will equal in number the tribes of the Israelites. [6]In the future, these are to be a sign among you. When your children ask you, 'What do these stones mean to you?' [7]you shall answer them, 'The waters of the Jordan ceased to flow before the ark of the covenant of the LORD when it crossed the Jordan.' Thus these stones are to serve as a perpetual memorial to the Israelites." [8]The twelve Israelites did as Joshua had commanded: they took up twelve stones from the Jordan riverbed as the LORD had said to Joshua, one for each of the tribes of the Israelites. They carried them along to the camp site, and there they placed them. [9]Joshua set up the twelve stones that had been in the Jordan riverbed on the spot where the priests stood who were carrying the ark of the covenant. They are there to this day.

[10]The priests carrying the ark stood in the Jordan riverbed until everything had been done that the LORD had commanded Joshua to tell the people, just as Moses had commanded Joshua. The people crossed over quickly, [11]and when all the people had completed the crossing, the ark of the LORD also crossed; and

the priests were now in front of them. [12]The Reubenites, Gadites, and half-tribe of Manasseh, armed, marched in the vanguard of the Israelites, as Moses had ordered. [13]About forty thousand troops, equipped for battle, crossed over before the LORD to the plains of Jericho for war.

[14]That day the LORD exalted Joshua in the sight of all Israel, and so during his whole life they feared him as they had feared Moses.

[15]Then the LORD said to Joshua: [16]Command the priests carrying the ark of the covenant to come up from the Jordan. [17]Joshua commanded the priests, "Come up from the Jordan," [18]and when the priests carrying the ark of the covenant of the LORD had come up from the Jordan riverbed, as the soles of their feet regained the dry ground, the waters of the Jordan resumed their course and as before overflowed all its banks.

[19]The people came up from the Jordan on the tenth day of the first month, and camped in Gilgal on the eastern limits of Jericho. [20]At Gilgal Joshua set up the twelve stones that had been taken from the Jordan, [21]saying to the Israelites, "In the future, when your children ask their parents, 'What do these stones mean?' [22]you shall inform them, 'Israel crossed the Jordan here on dry ground.' [23]For the LORD, your God, dried up the

---

tribes (Exod 24:4). It would also seem that two traditions are combined in this chapter, the one centering on the memorial stones at Gilgal, the other on the stones set up in the Jordan itself (4:9). The full complement of the people, including the military forces, then complete the crossing (4:10-13), with the Deuteronomist not failing to mention the cooperation of the three Transjordanian tribes (4:12).

Speculation centers on the historical character of the event and the possibility of an unforeseen landslide blocking the flow of water, thus

waters of the Jordan in front of you until you crossed over, just as the LORD, your God, had done at the Red Sea, drying it up in front of us until we crossed over, ²⁴in order that all the peoples of the earth may know that the hand of the LORD is mighty, and that you may fear the LORD, your God, forever."

5 **Rites at Gilgal.** ¹When all the kings of the Amorites to the west of the Jordan and all the kings of the Canaanites by the sea heard that the LORD had dried up the waters of the Jordan before the Israelites until they crossed over, their hearts melted and they were utterly dispirited because of the Israelites.

²On this occasion the LORD said to Joshua: Make flint knives and circumcise Israel for the second time. ³So Joshua made flint knives and circumcised the Israelites at Gibeath-haaraloth. ⁴This was

the reason for the circumcision: Of all the people who had come out of Egypt, every male of military age had died in the wilderness during the journey after they came out of Egypt. ⁵Though all the men who came out were circumcised, none of those born in the wilderness during the journey after the departure from Egypt were circumcised. ⁶Now the Israelites wandered forty years in the wilderness, until all the warriors among the people that came forth from Egypt died off because they had not listened to the voice of the LORD. For the LORD swore that he would not let them see the land he had sworn to their ancestors to give us, a land flowing with milk and honey. ⁷It was the children God raised up in their stead whom Joshua circumcised, for these were yet with foreskins, not having been circumcised on the

making the passage possible. Such a fortuitous occurrence at the right moment would retain its "miraculous" character. But beyond all of that is the recognition that this is primarily a theological statement, not historical replay. The ark is a clear sign of YHWH's ongoing protection of his people. The earlier crossing of the Red Sea and the Jordan passage form parallel brackets incorporating this central idea (4:23-24).

5:1-15 Arrival in Canaan

Three unrelated events are woven together with the exodus theme as the thread. These are the circumcision ritual (5:2-9), the Passover celebration (5:10-12), and the vision of the warrior God (5:13-15).

The battle lines are clearly drawn at the chapter's beginning (and the favorable outcome foreshadowed; 5:1). According to Jewish law only the circumcised could eat the Passover (Exod 12:43-49). In a stylized, even too tidy, presentation of the data, there were no circumcised Hebrews at this point since those who had departed Egypt were now deceased and the rite had never been performed on their sons (5:2-8). This called for a performance of the rite. Two theories are at work here to explain the site of this ritual, both centering around Gilgal. The first gives a popular explanation

journey. [8]When the circumcision of the entire nation was complete, they remained in camp where they were, until they recovered. [9]Then the LORD said to Joshua: Today I have removed the reproach of Egypt from you. Therefore the place is called Gilgal to the present day.

[10]While the Israelites were encamped at Gilgal on the plains of Jericho, they celebrated the Passover on the evening of the fourteenth day of the month. [11]On the day after the Passover they ate of the produce of the land in the form of unleavened cakes and parched grain. On that same day [12]after they ate of the produce of the land, the manna ceased. No longer was there manna for the Israelites, who that year ate of the yield of the land of Canaan.

Siege at Jericho. [13]While Joshua was near Jericho, he raised his eyes and saw one who stood facing him, drawn sword in hand. Joshua went up to him and asked, "Are you one of us or one of our enemies?" [14]He replied, "Neither. I am the commander of the army of the LORD: now I have come." Then Joshua fell down to the ground in worship, and said to him, "What has my lord to say to his servant?" [15]The commander of the army

---

for a site known as Gibeath-haaraioth, "hill of the foreskins" (5:2-4). This is, however, only loosely connected with Gilgal, even phonetically, but it may have been a more primitive name of the site. Another possible origin is more closely related to the sanctuary after the circumcision is completed and the pagan state of uncircumcision removed (5:8-9); "I have removed" or "rolled away" employs the Hebrew verb *gallothi* in a very free allusion to Gilgal. The actual meaning of Gilgal is probably related to a "circle of stones."

The ritual of a later time appears in the account of the Passover (5:10-12). *Pesah* or Passover was originally a nomadic or pastoral feast, centering on the killing and eating of the spring lamb; Unleavened Bread was an agricultural feast joined to Passover only after the period of occupation, with bread eaten in its pure unfermented state. Here by retrojection the combined ritual is remanded to the time of the crossing, just as had been done in relating the exodus experience itself (Exod 12). In addition, now that the land of plenty has been reached there is no need for the miraculous manna formerly provided.

The heavenly warrior who appears to Joshua (5:13-15) is clearly YHWH himself, visible to humankind only in some form of apparition (Gen 18). This is a replay of Moses' experience at the burning bush; the command to remove the sandals is practically identical (Exod 3:4-10). Gideon will have a similar experience (Judg 6). Again Joshua's status is elevated and the stage is set for the subsequent battle in which the "warrior God," the leader of the heavenly forces, is the protagonist.

of the LORD replied to Joshua, "Remove your sandals from your feet, for the place on which you are standing is holy." And Joshua did so.

6 ¹Now Jericho was in a state of siege because of the presence of the Israelites. No one left or entered. ²And to Joshua the LORD said: I have delivered Jericho, its king, and its warriors into your power. ³Have all the soldiers circle the city, marching once around it. Do this for six days, ⁴with seven priests carrying ram's horns ahead of the ark. On the seventh day march around the city seven times, and have the priests blow the horns. ⁵When they give a long blast on the ram's horns and you hear the sound of the horn, all the people shall shout aloud.

Standing now on covenant soil and with the sacred events of the past recaptured, the Hebrews are poised for the conquest.

6:1-27 The siege of Jericho

There is probably no other biblical battle that has attained the notoriety of Jericho. And yet it is a narrative beset with historical and literary problems. The first thing to note is that there was no battle. The city was besieged and the walls collapsed. In addition, few biblical sites have received as much archeological attention, even as late as the 1950s. Although much has been recovered, the evidence points to Jericho having been destroyed centuries before the Hebrew incursion. It seems clear that the Jericho which Joshua found was already in ruins.

There are a number of sources underlying the narrative, with overlapping inconsistencies. The ark for example, so important for the victory, receives no mention after verse 13. Was there one set of trumpeters or two (6:8-9, 13)? Was there a constant din in the horn blasts (6:13) or silence until the single blast gave the signal to shout (6:16, 20)? There are doublets as well, e.g., the shout of the people (6:16, 20) and the injunction to save Rahab (6:17, 22).

The account is primarily theological. That Canaan eventually became the land of the Hebrews is incontestable. That this was accomplished by the power and protection of YHWH is central to Israel's belief. This is all reflected in the conquest of Jericho. A city already in ruins could very well have become a symbol of the entire conquest. The account is more liturgical than military: the role of the ark (6:6), the priests with the trumpets (6:8), the procession around the city walls (6:7), the significant biblical number seven (6:13), and the shout of the people (6:20). The siege takes place with no military intervention. The Hebrews see the walls fall; they storm the city; and victory is theirs. This was accomplished because of their obedience to YHWH in every detail. No life was lost; no damage experienced.

The wall of the city will collapse, and the people shall attack straight ahead.

⁶Summoning the priests, Joshua, son of Nun, said to them, "Take up the ark of the covenant with seven of the priests carrying ram's horns in front of the ark of the LORD." ⁷And he ordered the people, "Proceed and surround the city, with the picked troops marching ahead of the ark of the LORD." ⁸When Joshua spoke to the people, the seven priests who carried the ram's horns before the LORD marched and blew their horns, and the ark of the covenant of the LORD followed them. ⁹In front of the priests with the horns marched the picked troops; the rear guard followed the ark, and the blowing of horns was kept up continually as they marched. ¹⁰But Joshua had commanded the people, "Do not shout or make any noise or outcry until I tell you, 'Shout!' Then you must shout." ¹¹So he had the ark of the LORD circle the city, going once around it, after which they returned to camp for the night.

¹²Early the next morning, Joshua had the priests take up the ark of the LORD. ¹³The seven priests bearing the ram's horns marched in front of the ark of the LORD, blowing their horns. Ahead of these marched the picked troops, while the rear guard followed the ark of the LORD, and the blowing of horns was kept up continually. ¹⁴On this second day they again marched around the city once before returning to camp; and for six days in all they did the same.

¹⁵On the seventh day, beginning at daybreak, they marched around the city seven times in the same manner; on that day only did they march around the city seven times. ¹⁶The seventh time around, the priests blew the horns and Joshua said to the people, "Now shout, for the LORD has given you the city. ¹⁷The city and everything in it is under the ban. Only Rahab the prostitute and all who are in the house with her are to live, because she hid the messengers we sent. ¹⁸But be careful not to covet or take anything that is under the ban; otherwise you will bring upon the camp of Israel this ban and the misery of it. ¹⁹All silver and gold, and the articles of bronze or iron, are holy to the LORD. They shall be put in the treasury of the LORD."

The Fall of Jericho. ²⁰As the horns blew, the people began to shout. When they heard the sound of the horn, they raised a tremendous shout. The wall collapsed, and the people attacked the city

---

The notion of *herem* or "the ban" is alien to modern thought (6:18-19). Evil was the antithesis of YHWH himself. Its force had to be eliminated or kept at a distance lest it affect God's people. Evil was seen as infectious and had to be rooted out (Deut 7:1-4); this meant people, livestock, and property (Deut 13:13-19). In the case of Jericho, only the precious metals were to be saved and placed in the sacred treasury, an anachronistic reference to the later constructed temple (6:19).

There are a number of etiologies in the narrative. The deliverance of Rahab and her family explained the later custom of allowing non-Israelite peoples to live in the community (6:22-24); the prohibition to rebuild Jericho

"The Wall [of Jericho] collapsed, and the people attacked the city straight ahead and took it" (Josh 6:20).

straight ahead and took it. ²¹They observed the ban by putting to the sword all living creatures in the city: men and women, young and old, as well as oxen, sheep and donkeys.

²² To the two men who had spied out the land, Joshua said, "Go into the prostitute's house and bring out the woman with all her family, as you swore to her you would do." ²³The spies entered and brought out Rahab, with her father, mother, brothers, and all her family; her entire family they led forth and placed outside the camp of Israel. ²⁴The city itself they burned with all that was in it; but the silver, gold, and articles of bronze and iron they placed in the treasury of the house of the LORD. ²⁵Because Rahab the prostitute had hidden the messengers whom Joshua had sent to reconnoiter Jericho, Joshua let her live,

along with her father's house and all her family, who dwell in the midst of Israel to this day.

²⁶On that occasion Joshua imposed the oath: Cursed before the LORD be the man who attempts to rebuild this city, Jericho. At the cost of his firstborn will he lay its foundation, and at the cost of his youngest son will he set up its gates.

²⁷Thus the LORD was with Joshua so that his fame spread throughout the land.

Defeat at Ai. ¹But the Israelites acted treacherously with regard to the ban; Achan, son of Carmi, son of Zabdi, son of Zerah of the tribe of Judah, took goods that were under the ban, and the anger of the LORD flared up against the Israelites.

²Joshua next sent men from Jericho to Ai, which is near Beth-aven and east of

---

alludes to the precept violated during the reign of Ahab (6:26; 1 Kgs 16:34); the central etiology probably explained the ruins of Jericho itself. If Jericho was already in ruins at the time of the occupation, it could well have taken on the symbolism of a fallen country. For this reason it was never to be rebuilt.

In their initial foray the Hebrews met an unqualified success, always by the power of YHWH, the "warrior God."

7:1-24 Defeat at Ai

The sin of Achan is related to the defeat and subsequent victory at Ai (ch. 8) but was probably originally an independent tradition. It tells the story of a single person's disobedience in taking goods that were under the ban (7:1; cf. 6:15-19), and the first defeat of the Hebrews as a result (7:2-9). The guilty man pays for the crime with his life and only then is the reproach lifted (7:16-24). The event may well have been originally associated with another time and place and later attached to the Ai campaign. It serves well the Deuteronomist's theme of inevitable punishment following upon evil.

Joshua's scouts are sent to reconnoiter sites in the interior and central part of the country, in the region of Bethel (7:2). This leads them to the city

Bethel, with the order, "Go up and reconnoiter the land." When they had explored Ai, ³they returned to Joshua and advised, "Do not send all the people up; if only about two or three thousand go up, they can attack and overcome Ai. You need not tire all the people: the enemy there are few." ⁴About three thousand of the people made the attack, but they fled before the army at Ai, ⁵who killed some thirty-six of them. They pursued them from the city gate to the Shebarim, and defeated them on the descent, so that the confidence of the people melted away like water.

⁶Joshua, together with the elders of Israel, tore their garments and fell face down before the ark of the LORD until evening; and they threw dust on their heads. ⁷"Alas, Lord GOD," Joshua prayed, "why did you ever allow this people to cross over the Jordan, delivering us into the power of the Amorites, that they might destroy us? Would that we had been content to dwell on the other side of the Jordan. ⁸Please, Lord, what can I say, now that Israel has turned its back to its enemies? ⁹When the Canaanites and the other inhabitants of the land hear of it, they will close in around us and efface our name from the earth. What will you do for your great name?"

¹⁰The LORD replied to Joshua: Stand up. Why are you lying there? ¹¹Israel has sinned: they have transgressed the covenant which I enjoined on them. They have taken goods subject to the ban. They have stolen and lied, placing the goods in their baggage. ¹²If the Israelites cannot stand up to their enemies, but must turn their back to them, it is because they are under the ban. I will not continue to be with you unless you remove that which is banned from among you. ¹³Get up, sanctify the people. Tell them, "Sanctify yourselves before tomorrow, for thus says the LORD, the God of Israel: That which is banned is in your midst, Israel. You cannot stand up to your enemies until you remove it from among you. ¹⁴In the morning you must come forward by tribes. The tribe which the LORD designates shall come forward by clans; the clan which the LORD designates shall come forward by families; the family which the LORD designates shall come forward one by one. ¹⁵Whoever is designated as having incurred the ban shall be destroyed by fire, with all that

---

of Ai and leads us to another historical quandary. Excavated in the last century, Ai, as its name signifies, was a long standing "ruin" by the time of the Hebrew invasion. Once again the name "Ruins" theologically suggests an important battle took place there. But the forces of Ai rout the Hebrews, killing thirty-six warriors and causing the first Israelite defeat (7:4-5).

This was a defeat viewed in ethical terms. Joshua is unable to explain the defeat (7:6-9), but YHWH explains it is due to moral default (7:10-15). In the theft of goods under the ban, the contagion of evil reached the people as a whole. Success will only come when the sin is excised at its core. The people must first go through purification rites (7:13; cf. 3:5), then through a process of elimination to determine the guilty party.

is his, because he has transgressed the covenant of the LORD and has committed a shameful crime in Israel."

Achan's Guilt and Punishment. [16]Early the next morning Joshua had Israel come forward by tribes, and the tribe of Judah was designated. [17]Then he had the clans of Judah come forward, and the clan of Zerah was designated. He had the clan of Zerah come forward by families, and Zabdi was designated. [18]Finally he had that family come forward one by one, and Achan, son of Carmi, son of Zabdi, son of Zerah of the tribe of Judah, was designated. [19]Joshua said to Achan, "My son, give glory to the LORD, the God of Israel, and praise him by telling me what you have done; do not hide it from me." [20]Achan answered Joshua, "I have indeed sinned against the LORD, the God of Israel. This is what I have done: [21]Among the spoils, I saw a beautiful Babylonian mantle, two hundred shekels of silver, and a bar of gold fifty shekels in weight; I coveted them and I took them. They are now hidden in the ground inside my tent, with the silver underneath." [22]Joshua sent messengers and they ran to the tent and there they were, hidden in the tent, with the silver underneath. [23]They took them from the tent, brought them to Joshua and all the Israelites, and spread them out before the LORD.

[24]Then Joshua and all Israel took Achan, son of Zerah, with the silver, the mantle, and the bar of gold, and with his sons and daughters, his ox, his donkey and his sheep, his tent, and all his possessions, and led them off to the Valley of Achor. [25]Joshua said, "What misery have you caused us? May the LORD bring misery upon you today!" And all Israel stoned him to death. They burnt them with fire and they stoned them. [26]Over Achan they piled a great heap of stones, which remains to the present day. Then the LORD turned from his anger. That is why the place is called the Valley of Achor to this day.

8 **Capture of Ai.**[1]The LORD then said to Joshua: Do not be afraid or dis-

---

By narrowing possibilities by tribe, clan, and family, in casting sacred lots (1 Sam 14:38-42), Achan emerges as the sinner (7:16-23). After the restoration of the sacred booty, he, along with his family and possessions, is taken away and stoned in a classic example of sin spreading its contagious net. The death not only of the culprit but his entire retinue is an example of solidarity in guilt.

A twofold significance is attached to the site of the death of Achan. His name is connected with the place, Achor (Hebrew for "misery"; cf. 7:25), and a heap of stones at the site recalling his death (7:26). This location later separated the territories of Benjamin and Judah, the latter being Achan's tribe of origin (7:1).

8:1-35 The conquest of Ai

At Jericho there had been no military action; at Ai, there is, with the capture centering on an ambush of the city. With moral guilt now removed,

mayed. Take all the army with you and prepare to attack Ai. I have delivered the king of Ai into your power, with his people, city, and land. ²Do to Ai and its king what you did to Jericho and its king—except that you may take its spoil and livestock as plunder. Set an ambush behind the city. ³So Joshua and all the soldiers prepared to attack Ai. Picking out thirty thousand warriors, Joshua sent them off by night ⁴with these orders: "See that you ambush the city from the rear. Do not be very far from the city. All of you must be ready. ⁵The rest of the people and I will come up to the city, and when they make a sortie against us as they did the last time, we will flee from them. ⁶They will keep coming out after us until we have drawn them away from the city, for they will think, 'They are fleeing from us as they did the last time.' When we flee, ⁷then you rise from ambush and take possession of the city, which the LORD, your God, will deliver into your power. ⁸When you have taken the city, set it on fire in obedience to the LORD's command. These are my orders to you." ⁹Then Joshua sent them away. They went to the place of ambush, taking up their position to the west of Ai, toward Bethel. Joshua, however, spent that night with the army.

¹⁰Early the next morning Joshua mustered the army and went up to Ai at its head, with the elders of Israel. ¹¹When all the troops he led were drawn up in position before the city, they pitched camp north of Ai, on the other side of the ravine. ¹²He took about five thousand warriors and set them in ambush between Bethel and Ai, west of the city. ¹³Thus the people took up their stations, with the main body north of the city and the ambush west of it, and Joshua waited overnight in the valley. ¹⁴The king of Ai saw this, and he and all his army came out very early in the morning to engage Israel in battle at the place in front of the Arabah, not knowing that there was an ambush behind the city. ¹⁵Joshua and the main body of the Israelites fled toward the wilderness, pretending defeat, ¹⁶until the last of the soldiers in the city had been called out to pursue them. Since they were drawn away from the city, with everyone pursuing Joshua, ¹⁷not a soldier remained in Ai or Bethel. They abandoned the city, leaving it open, as they pursued Israel.

¹⁸Then the LORD directed Joshua: Stretch out the javelin in your hand toward Ai, for I will deliver it into your power. Joshua stretched out the javelin in his hand toward the city, ¹⁹and as soon

---

victory is in the hands of the Israelites. At the Lord's injunction, the Hebrews are to destroy the city and its inhabitants. However, unlike Jericho, the ban is not total; booty is permitted from livestock and possessions (8:1-3). As happens frequently, the number of soldiers is evidently inflated (8:3; some texts read three thousand). Joshua gives orders for an ambush. Some troops are to remain concealed, while Joshua and his party draw the enemy forces out of the city. Once the city's forces have been sufficiently diminished, the concealed troops are to besiege and burn the stronghold (8:3-9).

as he did so, the men in ambush rose from their post, rushed in, captured the city, and immediately set it on fire. [20]By the time the army of Ai looked back, the smoke from the city was going up to the heavens. Escape in any direction was impossible, because the Israelites retreating toward the wilderness now turned on their pursuers; [21]for when Joshua and the main body of Israelites saw that the city had been taken by ambush and was going up in smoke, they struck back at the forces of Ai. [22]Since those in the city came out to intercept them, Ai's army was hemmed in by Israelites on both sides, who cut them down without any fugitives or survivors [23]except the king, whom they took alive and brought to Joshua.

[24]When Israel finished killing all the inhabitants of Ai in the open, who had pursued them into the wilderness, and

---

The tactic is executed exactly as planned (8:10-15). That victory belongs to the Lord is reflected in Joshua's extended javelin, a parallel to Moses' earlier posture during battle (8:18, 26; Exod 17:8-13). With the city destroyed and the booty taken, the dead king is exposed but only till sunset (Deut 21:22-23). His burial place remains a permanent reminder (8:29), just as the ruins of Ai speak permanently of the sacred conquest.

The historical problem present in the capture of Jericho appears again at Ai. If the settlement is to be identified with the present day el-Tell, a site slightly southeast of Bethel, as many scholars maintain, there is no support for its existence at the time of the conquest. The archeological findings indicate that it was destroyed in about 2000 B.C. and had a limited resettlement for about two centuries after 1200 B.C. The occupation at that later time may well have been Israelite, or more specifically Benjaminite.

The Joshua narrative, then, would be largely based on the end result of the conquest. It would have been composed as a composite of historical memories dealing with various battles and etiologies connected with important sites. It is also suggested that a later Israelite presence there would have found its justification in the limitations placed on the destruction of property in the story (8:1-2). Joshua then became the over-arching victor with his javelin extended in Moses-like fashion.

The ceremonial conclusion (8:30-35) carries out the injunction of Moses (Deut 27) and is clearly Deuteronomistic in character. If historically accurate it would posit a major jump into Canaanite territory some twenty miles to the north. It may actually date from a later time; it takes place in the region of Shechem, the place of covenant renewal in chapter 24. Shechem, standing between Mt. Ebal and Mt. Gerizim, is where this ceremony seems to have taken place (see v. 33) rather than on Mt. Ebal (8:30). There is an altar constructed from uncut stone (Exod 20:25), a sacrifice, and the reading of the law (8:30-35).

all of them to the last man fell by the sword, then all Israel returned and put to the sword those inside the city. ²⁵There fell that day a total of twelve thousand men and women, the entire population of Ai. ²⁶Joshua kept the javelin in his hand stretched out until he had carried out the ban on all the inhabitants of Ai. ²⁷However, the Israelites took for themselves as plunder the livestock and the spoil of that city, according to the command of the LORD issued to Joshua. ²⁸Then Joshua destroyed Ai by fire, reducing it to an everlasting mound of ruins, as it remains today. ²⁹He had the king of Ai hanged on a tree until evening; then at sunset Joshua ordered the body removed from the tree and cast at the entrance of the city gate, where a great heap of stones was piled up over it, which remains to the present day.

Altar on Mount Ebal. ³⁰Later, on Mount Ebal, Joshua built to the LORD, the God of Israel, an altar ³¹of unhewn stones on which no iron tool had been used, just as Moses, the servant of the LORD, had commanded the Israelites, as recorded in the book of the law. On this altar they sacrificed burnt offerings to the LORD and made communion sacrifices. ³²There, in the presence of the Israelites, Joshua inscribed upon the stones a copy of the law written by Moses. ³³And all Israel, resident alien and native alike, with their elders, officers and judges, stood on either side of the ark facing the levitical priests who were carrying the ark of the covenant of the LORD. Half of them were facing Mount Gerizim and half Mount Ebal, just as Moses, the servant of the LORD, had first commanded for the blessing of the people of Israel. ³⁴Then were read aloud all the words of the law, the blessings and the curses, exactly as written in the book of the law. ³⁵Every single word that Moses had commanded, Joshua read aloud to the entire assembly, including the women and children, and the resident aliens among them.

9 **Confederacy Against Israel.** ¹When the news reached all the kings west of the Jordan, in the mountain regions and in the Shephelah, and all along the coast of the Great Sea as far as the Lebanon: Hittites, Amorites, Canaanites,

---

The reading of the law is strongly Deuteronomistic in fulfilling the directive of Deuteronomy 27. At this religious high point, Joshua and all the people assemble in the presence of the ark to offer sacrifice and listen to the law of the Lord. There are the blessings and curses (8:34; Deut 28); more than simple utterances, they are truly effective instruments of prosperity or destruction.

9:1-27 The alliance with Gibeon

The dealings at Gibeon bring the Israelites into the central hill country. It lay only ten miles north of Jerusalem. It appears repeatedly in the Old Testament as one of the cities of Benjamin (18:25); it was a Levitical city (21:17) and the scene of warfare in the time of Samuel (2 Sam 2:12-16; 20:4-13). It became an important cultic site by the time of Solomon (1 Kgs 3:4).

Perizzites, Hivites, and Jebusites, ²they gathered together to launch a common attack against Joshua and Israel.

The Gibeonite Deception. ³On hearing what Joshua had done to Jericho and Ai, the inhabitants of Gibeon ⁴formed their own scheme. They chose provisions for a journey, making use of old sacks for their donkeys, and old wineskins, torn and mended. ⁵They wore old, patched sandals and shabby garments; and all the bread they took was dry and crumbly. ⁶Thus they journeyed to Joshua in the camp at Gilgal, where they said to him and to the Israelites, "We have come from a far-off land; now, make a covenant with us." ⁷But the Israelites replied to the Hivites, "You may be living in land that is ours. How, then, can we make a covenant with you?" ⁸But they answered Joshua, "We are your servants." Then Joshua asked them, "Who are you? Where do you come from?" ⁹They answered him, "Your servants have come from a far-off land, because of the fame of the LORD, your God. For we have heard reports of all that he did in Egypt ¹⁰and all that he did to the two kings of the Amorites beyond the Jordan, Sihon, king of Heshbon, and Og, king of Bashan, who lived in Ashtaroth. ¹¹So our elders and all the inhabitants of our land said to us, 'Take along provisions for the journey and go to meet them. Say to them: "We are your servants; now make a covenant with us."' ¹²This bread of ours was still warm when we brought it from home as provisions

---

This chapter contains the Gibeonite ruse to deceive Joshua (9:1-15) and the subordination treaty made with them. A number of etiologies come into play. It explains how this part of the central hill country came into Israelite control. Like the story of Rahab, it explains the peaceful co-existence between Israel and certain foreign peoples, despite the order of extermination (Deut 7:1-2). Joshua is the central figure (9:6, 8, 15), with another tradition highlighting the community leaders (9:7, 14, 16). Although Gibeon is central, other cities are mentioned as well. Even though certain features of the deception strain its credibility, the story is well told. The reference to the Gibeonites as Hivites relates them to a larger ethnic body; at another point they are also termed Amorites (2 Sam 21:2). They are presented as being conversant with past Hebrew victories in the Transjordan. Disguised as poor exhausted foreigners, the Gibeonites succeed handily in deception (9:12-15), but not without the ironic surmise of the Israelites: "You may be living in land that is ours" (9:7).

A treaty once made is irrevocable. Thus, there is nothing to be done now except to spare the Gibeonites. Fortunately for Israel the treaty offered minimum benefits, only life itself. Nothing precluded the Gibeonites from being relegated to an inferior social class, as choppers of wood and bearers of water for the community and the sanctuary (9:27). From their designated state there would be no escape (9:23), even though they were

the day we left to come to you, but now it is dry and crumbly. [13]Here are our wineskins, which were new when we filled them, but now they are torn. Look at our garments and sandals; they are worn out from the very long journey." [14]Then the Israelite leaders partook of their provisions, without inquiring of the LORD. [15]So Joshua made peace with them and made a covenant to let them live, which the leaders of the community sealed with an oath.

Gibeonites Made Vassals. [16]Three days after the covenant was made, the Israelites heard that these people were from nearby, and would be living in Israel. [17]The third day on the road, the Israelites came to their cities of Gibeon, Chephirah, Beeroth, and Kiriath-jearim, [18]but did not attack them, because the leaders of the community had sworn to them by the LORD, the God of Israel. When the entire community grumbled against the leaders, [19]these all remonstrated with the community, "We have sworn to them by the LORD, the God of Israel, and so we cannot harm them. [20]Let us therefore let them live, and so deal with them that no wrath fall upon us because of the oath we have sworn to them." [21]Thus the leaders said to them, "Let them live, and become hewers of wood and drawers of water for the entire community." So the community did as the leaders advised them.

[22]Joshua summoned the Gibeonites and said to them, "Why did you deceive us and say, 'We live far off from you'?—You live among us! [23]Now are you accursed: every one of you shall always be a slave, hewers of wood and drawers of water, for the house of my God." [24]They answered Joshua, "Your servants were fully informed of how the LORD, your God, commanded Moses his servant that you be given the entire land and that all its inhabitants be destroyed before you. Since, therefore, at your advance, we were in great fear for our lives, we acted as we did. [25]And now that we are in your power, do with us what is good and right in your eyes." [26]Joshua did what he had decided: while he saved them from being killed by the Israelites, [27]on that day he made them, as they still are, hewers of wood and drawers of water for the community and for the altar of the LORD, in the place the LORD would choose.

10 **The Siege of Gibeon.** [1]Now when Adonizedek, king of Jerusalem, heard that Joshua had captured Ai and put it under the ban, and had done to that city and its king as he had done to Jericho and its king, and that the

---

to live peaceably in the Hebrew community. In fact, violent action against the Gibeonites in monarchical times was seen as a serious covenant violation (2 Sam 21:1-6).

10:1-43 The Southern campaign

The chapter contains three originally unconnected accounts: the siege of Gibeon (9:1-15), the death of the five kings (9:15-27), and the invasion of southern Palestine (9:28-43). Their original separation with resultant overlapping does not detract from the author's intent of placing the land as far south as the Negeb in Israelite hands.

inhabitants of Gibeon had made their peace with Israel, remaining among them, ²there was great fear abroad, because Gibeon was a great city, like one of the royal cities, greater even than Ai, and all its men were warriors. ³So Adonizedek, king of Jerusalem, sent to Hoham, king of Hebron, Piram, king of Jarmuth, Japhia, king of Lachish, and Debir, king of Eglon, with this message: ⁴"Come and help me attack Gibeon, for it has made peace with Joshua and the Israelites." ⁵The five Amorite kings, of Jerusalem, Hebron, Jarmuth, Lachish, and Eglon, gathered with all their forces, and marched against Gibeon to make war on it. ⁶Thereupon, the Gibeonites sent an appeal to Joshua in his camp at Gilgal: "Do not abandon your servants. Come up here quickly and save us. Help us, because all the Amorite kings of the mountain country have joined together against us."

Joshua's Victory. ⁷So Joshua marched up from Gilgal with all his army and all his warriors. ⁸The Lord said to Joshua: Do not fear them, for I have delivered them into your power. Not one of them will be able to withstand you. ⁹After an all-night march from Gilgal, Joshua made a surprise attack upon them, ¹⁰and the Lord threw them into disorder before Israel. The Israelites inflicted a great slaughter on them at Gibeon and pursued them down the Beth-horon slope, attacking them as far as Azekah and Makkedah.

¹¹While they fled before Israel along the descent of Beth-horon, the Lord hurled great stones from the heavens above them all the way to Azekah, killing many. More died from these hailstones than the Israelites killed with the sword. ¹²It was then, when the Lord delivered up the Amorites to the Israelites, that Joshua prayed to the Lord, and said in the presence of Israel:

10:1-11 War at Gibeon

When the treaty with the Gibeonites reached royal ears, the king of Jerusalem enlisted the help of four other kings to attack Gibeon (10:1-4). The Amorite cities of Jarmuth, Hebron, Lachish, and Eglon were situated to the south of Jerusalem, all seen as closely related to Judah in later times. Faced with this grave danger, the Gibeonites logically looked to their covenant partner, Israel, for help. With the Deuteronomistic assurance of success, Joshua sets forth with his troops (10:7-8). They have an unparalleled victory and relentlessly pursue their enemy. Divine assistance provides a storm of hail which causes more damage than the human battle (10:11).

The quotation from the book of Jashar, a record of Israel's mighty deeds (10:12-13; 2 Sam 1:18), originally commanded an "astonished" sun and moon to stand still before God's might. The quotation is often interpreted as a plea for the prolongation of daylight. However it is better seen as a plea for the darkness to continue, with the sun obscured by the hailstorm. The darkness worked to the advantage of Israel in overcoming the enemy.

Sun, stand still at Gibeon,
> Moon, in the valley of Aijalon!

[13]The sun stood still,
> the moon stayed,
> while the nation took vengeance
> on its foes.

This is recorded in the Book of Jashar. The sun halted halfway across the heavens; not for an entire day did it press on. [14]Never before or since was there a day like this, when the LORD obeyed the voice of a man; for the LORD fought for Israel. [15]Then Joshua and all Israel returned to the camp at Gilgal.

Execution of Amorite Kings. [16]The five kings who had fled hid in the cave at Makkedah. [17]When Joshua was told, "The five kings have been found, hiding in the cave at Makkedah," [18]he said, "Roll large stones to the mouth of the cave and post guards over it. [19]But do not remain there yourselves. Pursue your enemies, and harry them in the rear. Do not allow them to reach their cities, for the LORD, your God, has delivered them into your power."

[20]Once Joshua and the Israelites had finally inflicted the last blows in this very great slaughter, and the survivors had escaped from them into the fortified cities, [21]all the army returned to Joshua and the camp at Makkedah in victory; no one uttered a sound against the Israelites. [22]Then Joshua said, "Open the mouth of the cave and bring me those five kings from the cave." [23]They did so; they brought out to him from the cave the five kings, of Jerusalem, Hebron, Jarmuth, Lachish, and Eglon. [24]When they brought the five kings out to Joshua, he summoned all the army of Israel and said to the commanders of the soldiers who had marched with him, "Come forward and put your feet on the necks of these kings." They came forward and put their feet upon their necks. [25]Then Joshua said to them, "Do not be afraid or dismayed, be firm and steadfast. This is what the LORD will do to all the enemies against whom you fight." [26]Thereupon Joshua struck and killed the kings, and hanged them on five trees, where they remained hanging until evening. [27]At sunset Joshua commanded that they be taken down from the trees and be thrown into the cave where they had hidden; over the mouth of the cave large stones were placed, which remain until this very day.

Conquest of Southern Canaan. [28]Makkedah, too, Joshua captured and put to the sword at that time. He put the city, its king, and every person in it under the ban, leaving no survivors. Thus he did to the king of Makkedah what he had done to the king of Jericho. [29]Joshua then passed on with all Israel from Makkedah to Libnah, and attacked it, [30]and the LORD

10:16-27 The murder of the kings

The murder of the kings at Makkedah is etiological, with the presence of the memorial stones commemorating their death. The kings were left concealed in caves until the battle was finished (10:16-19). They are killed only after suffering the humiliation of having their necks stamped upon (10:24; Ps 110:1). With their death and public exposure until sunset (10:26; Deut 21:22-23), Israel's victory is definitively assured.

delivered it, with its king, into the power of Israel. He put it to the sword with every person there, leaving no survivors. Thus he did to its king what he had done to the king of Jericho. ³¹Joshua next passed on with all Israel from Libnah to Lachish, where they set up a camp during the attack. ³²The LORD delivered Lachish into the power of Israel, so that on the second day Joshua captured it and put it to the sword with every person in it, just as he had done to Libnah. ³³At that time Horam, king of Gezer, came up to help Lachish, but Joshua defeated him and his people, leaving him no survivors. ³⁴From Lachish, Joshua passed on with all Israel to Eglon; encamping near it, they attacked it ³⁵and captured it the same day, putting it to the sword. On that day he put under the ban every person in it, just as he had done at Lachish. ³⁶From Eglon, Joshua went up with all Israel to Hebron, which they attacked ³⁷and captured. They put it to the sword with its king, all its cities, and every person there, leaving no survivors, just as

Joshua had done to Eglon. He put it under the ban and every person in it. ³⁸Then Joshua and all Israel turned back to Debir and attacked it, ³⁹capturing it with its king and all its cities. They put them to the sword and put under the ban every person in it, leaving no survivors. Thus he did to Debir and its king what he had done to Hebron, as well as to Libnah and its king.

⁴⁰Joshua conquered the entire land; the mountain regions, the Negeb, the Shephelah, and the mountain slopes, with all their kings. He left no survivors, but put under the ban every living being, just as the LORD, the God of Israel, had commanded. ⁴¹Joshua conquered them from Kadesh-barnea to Gaza, and all the land of Goshen to Gibeon. ⁴²All these kings and their lands Joshua captured all at once, for the LORD, the God of Israel, fought for Israel. ⁴³Thereupon Joshua with all Israel returned to the camp at Gilgal.

11 Northern Confederacy. ¹When Jabin, king of Hazor, learned of

---

10:28-42 The conquest of the South

This is primarily a list of the sites taken by Israel in settling in southern Palestine, many of which attained notoriety in later history. Those conquered are Libnah, Lachish, Gezer, Eglon, and Debir, all belonging to the tribe of Judah (15:39-44). This is a summary list with no indication of the time it took to assimilate the entire region from the central hill country to the southern Negeb desert. Not all of the cities included in the original hostile coalition are mentioned, e.g., Jerusalem and Jarmuth. Jerusalem was not taken until David's time (2 Sam 5:6-9). *Herem* (the ban) is dutifully executed on the whole region. At this point Joshua is clearly seen as an agent of the Lord, bringing the country into subjection in what is presented as a "blitzkrieg" attack.

11:1-25 The Northern campaign

This chapter is thematic in character, painting in broad strokes a conquest of the north of Canaan which even other biblical sources indicate took

"Joshua . . . captured Hazor and struck down its king with the sword;
for Hazor was the chief of all those kingdoms" (Josh 11:10).
The archaeological remains of Tel Hazor are the richest and largest in modern Israel.

this, he sent a message to Jobab, king of Madon, to the king of Shimron, to the king of Achshaph, ²and to the northern kings in the mountain regions and in the Arabah near Chinneroth, in the Shephelah, and in Naphath-dor to the west. ³These were Canaanites to the east and west, Amorites, Hittites, Perizzites, and Jebusites in the mountain regions, and Hivites at the foot of Hermon in the land of Mizpah. ⁴They came out with all their troops, an army numerous as the sands on the seashore, and with a multitude of horses and chariots. ⁵All these kings made a pact and together they marched to the waters of Merom, where they encamped to fight against Israel.

⁶The LORD said to Joshua, "Do not fear them, for by this time tomorrow I will present them slain to Israel. You must hamstring their horses and burn their chariots." ⁷Joshua with his whole army came upon them suddenly at the waters of Merom and fell upon them. ⁸The LORD delivered them into the power of the Israelites, who defeated them and pursued them to Greater Sidon, to Misrephoth-maim, and eastward to the valley of Mizpeh. They struck them all down, leaving no survivors. ⁹Joshua did to them as the LORD had commanded: he hamstrung their horses and burned their chariots.

Conquest of Northern Canaan. ¹⁰At that time Joshua, turning back, captured Hazor and struck down its king with the sword; for Hazor formerly was the chief of all those kingdoms. ¹¹He also struck down with the sword every person there, carrying out the ban, till none was

---

a much longer time. This is theological history which has to be understood on its own terms. The chapter existed as an independent and separate source, now utilized by the Deuteronomist to match his overall purpose. Except for the reference to Jabin's hearing of the southern campaign (11:1), there is no other reference to preceding events. The two time references (11:10, 21) are vague and are not necessarily sequential. The chapter is made up of three main sections: the formation of a confederacy (11:1-9), similar to that of the south (9:1-2); the battle (11:10-15); and a survey of the conquest (11:16-23). All of these have their parallel in the southern campaign.

11:1-9 The Northern confederacy

The fear of the Israelites moves the northern kings to form a confederacy. Hazor is north of the Sea of Galilee (Genesareth), a prominent city in the Middle Bronze era, and impressive ruins in later times. It was rebuilt in the time of Solomon (1 Kgs 9:15). Madon is identified with a site also close to the Sea of Galilee, while the cities of Shimron and Achshaph cannot be identified with certainty (11:1-2). The list of tribal peoples inhabiting the north corresponds to what is known from other sources; only the presence of the southern (Jerusalem-inhabiting) Jebusites is rather surprising (11:3). The actual location of Merom, the place of battle, remains enigmatic, other

left alive. Hazor itself he burned. ¹²All the cities of those kings, and the kings themselves, Joshua captured and put to the sword, carrying out the ban on them, as Moses, the servant of the Lord, had commanded. ¹³However, Israel did not destroy by fire any of the cities built on their mounds, except Hazor, which Joshua burned. ¹⁴All the spoil and livestock of these cities the Israelites took as plunder; but the people they put to the sword, until they had destroyed the last of them, leaving none alive. ¹⁵As the Lord had commanded his servant Moses, so Moses commanded Joshua, and Joshua acted accordingly. He left nothing undone that the Lord had commanded Moses should be done.

Survey of the Conquest. ¹⁶So Joshua took all this land: the mountain regions, the entire Negeb, all the land of Goshen, the Shephelah, the Arabah, as well as the mountain regions and Shephelah of Israel, ¹⁷from Mount Halak that rises toward Seir as far as Baal-gad in the Lebanon valley at the foot of Mount Hermon. All their kings he captured and put to death. ¹⁸Joshua waged war against all these kings for a long time. ¹⁹With the exception of the Hivites who lived in Gibeon, no city made peace with the Israelites; all were taken in battle. ²⁰For it was the Lord's doing to make their hearts obstinate to meet Israel in battle, that they might be put under the ban without mercy, and be destroyed as the Lord had commanded Moses.

²¹At that time Joshua penetrated the mountain regions and exterminated the Anakim in Hebron, Debir, Anab, the entire mountain region of Judah, and the entire mountain region of Israel. Joshua

---

than its general location in the upper Galilee region (11:5). Following the Lord's directives exactly, the Israelites cripple their enemies' defense, pursue them to the far north, and then kill them all (11:6-9).

11:10-15 Conquest of Northern Canaan

After the defeat of the armed forces, the Israelites turn on the cities themselves. The entire population is eradicated; the city of Hazor is put to the torch; the spoils and livestock are taken as booty. This is *herem* at its strongest, enjoined on Moses by the Lord himself (Deut 7:2). It can only be understood against the background of the pernicious and contagious properties of evil, calling for a type of total eradication foreign to the modern ear. It also underscores the invincibility of yhwh in the face of any pagan threat.

11:16-23 Survey of the conquest

Joshua's conquest is idealized here and is more reflective of events that only came about gradually, as verse 18 indicates. The boundaries extend from the Negeb in the far south to the northern-most point of Mt. Hermon. The conquest goes much farther than anything seen so far, with some territories, still unconquered, appearing later in the book itself (13:1-6; 15:63; 16:10). There are forays against foreign inhabitants still flourishing in the

put them and their cities under the ban, [22]so that no Anakim were left in the land of the Israelites. However, some survived in Gaza, in Gath, and in Ashdod. [23]Thus Joshua took the whole land, just as the LORD had said to Moses. Joshua gave it to Israel as their heritage, apportioning it among the tribes. And the land had rest from war.

12 **Lists of Conquered Kings.** [1]These are the kings of the land whom the Israelites conquered and whose lands they occupied, east of the Jordan, from the River Arnon to Mount Hermon, including all the eastern section of the Arabah: [2]First, Sihon, king of the Amorites, who lived in Heshbon. His domain extended from Aroer, which is on the bank of the Wadi Arnon, to include the wadi itself, and the land northward through half of Gilead to the Wadi Jabbok at the border with the Ammonites, [3]as well as the Arabah from the eastern side of the Sea of Chinnereth, as far south as the eastern side of the Salt Sea of the Arabah in the direction of Beth-jeshimoth, southward under the slopes of Pisgah. [4]Secondly, the border of Og, king of Bashan, a survivor of the Rephaim, who lived at Ashtaroth and Edrei. [5]He ruled over Mount Hermon, Salecah, and all Bashan as far as the boundary of the Geshurites and Maacathites, and over half of Gilead as far as the territory of Sihon, king of Heshbon. [6]It was Moses, the servant of the LORD, and the Israelites who conquered them; Moses, the servant of the LORD, gave possession of their land to the Reubenites, the Gadites, and the half-tribe of Manasseh.

[7]This is a list of the kings of the land whom Joshua and the Israelites conquered west of the Jordan, from Baal-gad in the Lebanon valley to Mount Halak which rises toward Seir; Joshua apportioned their land and gave possession of it to the tribes of Israel; [8]it included the mountain regions and Shephelah, the Arabah, the slopes, the wilderness, and the Negeb, belonging to the Hittites, Amorites, Canaanites, Perizzites, Hivites,

---

time of the Judges. The total elimination of the Anakim (v. 22) is at odds with their later presence in the territory of Caleb (14:6-15; 15:13-19).

Divine causality is overarching in biblical thought. It was YHWH who hardened pharaoh's heart (Exod 7:13) so that the liberating plagues might take place. Here too the Lord encourages the enemy to wage war so that they may be justifiably defeated and not killed as innocent landowners (11:20). With nothing happening without his authorization, the Lord manages "to write straight with crooked lines."

12:1-24 Summary of the conquest

This chapter links the two major sections of the book, the conquest and the distribution of the land. It has two parts, one dealing with the taking of the land east of the Jordan under Moses (12:1-6), the other, with the victories of Joshua (12:7-24). The first is more broadly geographical; the second, centering on the royal fiefdoms overcome.

and Jebusites: ⁹The king of Jericho, one; the king of Ai, which is near Bethel, one; ¹⁰the king of Jerusalem, one; the king of Hebron, one; ¹¹the king of Jarmuth, one; the king of Lachish, one; ¹²the king of Eglon, one; the king of Gezer, one; ¹³the king of Debir, one; the king of Geder, one; ¹⁴the king of Hormah, one; the king of Arad, one; ¹⁵the king of Libnah, one; the king of Adullam, one; ¹⁶the king of Makkedah, one; the king of Bethel, one; ¹⁷the king of Tappuah, one; the king of Hepher, one; ¹⁸the king of Aphek, one; the king of Lasharon, one; ¹⁹the king of Madon, one; the king of Hazor, one; ²⁰the king of Shimron, one; the king of Achshaph, one; ²¹the king of Taanach, one; the king of Megiddo, one; ²²the king of Kedesh, one; the king of Jokneam, at Carmel, one; ²³the king of Dor, in Naphathdor, one; the king of Goyim at Gilgal, one; ²⁴and the king of Tirzah, one—thirty-one kings in all.

II. Division of the Land

13 **Division of Land Commanded.** ¹When Joshua was old and advanced in years, the LORD said to him: Though now you are old and advanced in years, a very large part of the land still

The account of the Hebrew victory over Sihon, king of the Amorites, and Og, king of Bashan, is found in Numbers 21:21-35. From south to north in the land east of the Jordan, the territory extended from the Arnon River at the Dead Sea to Mt. Hermon in the far north (12:1). The territory of the two kings was divided by the Jabbok river, Sihon being the king to the south with his capital at Heshbon (12:2-3), and Og ruling in the north (12:4-6). Legend had the people of Bashan as being tall of stature, hence the Rephaim (12:4; i.e., "giants").

The significance of recounting the capture of Bashan and Og lies in the fact that the Israelite tribes of Reuben, Gad, and one half of Manasseh were allotted that territory at the time of distribution (ch. 13).

The territories west of the Jordan are succinctly enumerated, with a simple mention of the kings and their land. Some of these locations are already known to us from Joshua itself or from other sources; others are not. The evidence points to an early independent source used and adapted by the Deuteronomist, whose imprint is present in the sequence and ordering of the names. In addition to Jericho and Ai, there are the five cities listed in 10:3 (12:10-12) and the four of 11:1 (12:19-20).

While it is not possible to identify each of the cities with certainty, those which are known extend to the farthest points of Canaan in the south and north. The chapter is a tribute to the leadership of Moses and Joshua. It points to the end of petty fiefdoms and the emergence of a theocratic and unified country with a clear religious, if not yet national, identity. It will have its finest hour under David in a lifespan that was destined to be all too short.

remains to be possessed. ²This is the remaining land: all Geshur and all the districts of the Philistines ³(from the stream adjoining Egypt to the boundary of Ekron in the north is reckoned Canaanite territory, though held by the five lords of the Philistines in Gaza, Ashdod, Ashkelon, Gath, and Ekron); ⁴also where the Avvim are in the south; all the land of the Canaanites from Mearah of the Sidonians to Aphek, and the boundaries of the Amorites; ⁵and the Gebalite territory; and all the Lebanon on the east, from Baal-gad at the foot of Mount Hermon to Lebo-hamath. ⁶All the inhabitants of the mountain regions between Lebanon and Misrephoth-maim, all Sidonians, I will drive out before the Israelites; at least include these areas in the division of the Israelite heritage, just as I have commanded you. ⁷Now, therefore, apportion among the nine tribes and the half-tribe of Manasseh the land which is to be their heritage.

DIVISION OF THE LAND

Joshua 13–21

Following upon the rather idealized picture of Joshua's conquest of Canaan, the second major part of the book deals with the allotment of the land, bringing to a conclusion the objective enunciated by Moses (11:23). This begins with the land east of the Jordan, promised to two and one-half tribes (13:8-32; Num 32:32-33), with the territory in Canaan itself given to the remaining eight and one-half tribes (chs. 14–20). In addition, there is added clarification of the special status of the tribe of Levi (ch. 21). Due to the limitations of space, and possibly reader interest as well, geographical detail is absent here, for which the reader is directed to lengthier and more critical commentaries. These chapters have special interest for the Deuteronomist in reminding his readers, at a much later date and in a time of dispersion and disappointment, of the truly felicitous conclusion to the exodus, a realization of promise, which was initially theirs.

13:1-7 Land to be conquered

This is a touch of realism brought to an idealized presentation of the land's possession. There were still pockets of resistance, some of which were to continue into monarchical times. The territory mentioned here includes the coastal land of the Philistines with its five major cities (13:2-3), which remained hostile and inimical well into the time of David (2 Sam 5:17-24), and the Geshurites (2 Sam 27:8), a people distinct from the Transjordanian group of the same name (12:3). Mention is also made of northern Canaanites, near Amorite country (13:4), and a territory further north in the Lebanon region (13:5). These are presented as part of Israel's heritage, although still unconquered in the time of Joshua (13:6).

The Eastern Tribes. [8]Now the other half of the tribe of Manasseh, as well as the Reubenites and Gadites, had taken as their heritage what Moses, the servant of the LORD, had given them east of the Jordan: [9]from Aroer on the bank of the Wadi Arnon and the city in the wadi itself, through the tableland of Medeba and Dibon, [10]with the rest of the cities of Sihon, king of the Amorites, who reigned in Heshbon, to the boundary of the Ammonites; [11]also Gilead and the territory of the Geshurites and Maacathites, all Mount Hermon, and all Bashan as far as Salecah, [12]the entire kingdom in Bashan of Og, who was king at Ashtaroth and Edrei (he was a holdover from the remnant of the Rephaim). These Moses defeated and dispossessed. [13]But the Israelites did not dispossess the Geshurites and Maacathites, so that Geshur and Maacath dwell in the midst of Israel to this day. [14]However, Moses assigned no heritage to the tribe of Levi; the LORD, the God of Israel, is their heritage, as the LORD had promised them.

Reuben. [15]This is what Moses gave to the tribe of the Reubenites by their clans: [16]Their territory reached from Aroer, on the bank of the Wadi Arnon, and the city in the wadi itself, through the tableland about Medeba, [17]to include Heshbon and all its towns on the tableland, Dibon, Bamoth-baal, Beth-baal-meon, [18]Jahaz, Kedemoth, Mephaath, [19]Kiriathaim, Sibmah, Zereth-shahar on the knoll within the valley, [20]Beth-peor, the slopes of Pisgah, Beth-jeshimoth, [21]and the other cities of the tableland and of the whole kingdom of Sihon. This Amorite king, who reigned in Heshbon, Moses had defeated, with the princes of Midian, vassals of Sihon who were settled in the land: Evi, Rekem, Zur, Hur, and Reba; [22]Balaam, son of Beor, the diviner, the Israelites killed with the sword, together with those they struck down. [23]The boundary of the Reubenites was the Jordan. These cities and their villages were the heritage of the Reubenites by their clans.

Gad. [24]This is what Moses gave to the tribe of the Gadites by their clans: [25]Their territory included Jazer, all the cities of Gilead, and half the land of the Ammonites as far as Aroer, toward Rabbah [26](that is, from Heshbon to Ramath-mizpeh and Betonim, and from Mahanaim to the boundary of Lo-debar); [27]and in the Jordan valley: Beth-haram, Beth-nimrah, Succoth, Zaphon, the other part of the kingdom of Sihon, king of Heshbon, with

13: 8-29 The Eastern tribes

Once again the tribes to which Moses had assigned territory in Transjordan—Reuben, Gad, and one-half of Manasseh—are highlighted (12:6; Num 32:32). The allotment moves from south to north: Reuben's is the land between the Arnon river and the region of Heshbon, slightly north of the Dead Sea (13:15-23). This was the land of the Amorites with its former king Sihon, recalled here for its association with Moses (Num 21:21-31).

Gad is allotted the region beyond Heshbon which was part of Ammon and Gilead in northern Transjordan (13:24-25). Its northern boundary is not clear from the text since most of the cities mentioned cannot be identified

the bank of the Jordan to the southeastern tip of the Sea of Chinnereth. ²⁸These cities and their villages were the heritage of the clans of the Gadites.

Manasseh. ²⁹This is what Moses gave to the half-tribe of Manasseh; the half-tribe of the Manassites, by their clans, had ³⁰territory including Mahanaim, all of Bashan, the entire kingdom of Og, king of Bashan, and all the villages of Jair, which are sixty cities in Bashan. ³¹Half of Gilead, with Ashtaroth and Edrei, royal cities of Og in Bashan, fell to the descendants of Machir, son of Manasseh, to half the Machirites, by their clans.

³²These are the heritages which Moses gave when he was in the plains of Moab, beyond the Jordan east of Jericho. ³³But Moses gave no heritage to the tribe of Levi: the LORD, the God of Israel, is their heritage, as he had promised them.

14 **The Western Tribes.** ¹These are the portions which the Israelites received as heritage in the land of Canaan. Eleazar the priest, Joshua, son of Nun, and the heads of families in the tribes of the Israelites determined ²their heritage by lot, as the LORD had commanded through Moses concerning the remaining nine and a half tribes. ³To two and a half tribes Moses had already given a heritage beyond the Jordan; to the Levites he had given no heritage among them: ⁴the descendants of Joseph formed two tribes, Manasseh and Ephraim. But the Levites were given no share of the land except cities to live in, with their pasture lands for the herds and flocks.

---

with certainty. Manasseh receives Bashan, the land of Og (Num 21:33-35), including a part of Gilead (13:29-31). In summary, the Transjordanian tribes occupied a territory extending roughly from the Dead Sea in the south to the Lake of Chinnereth in the north, although the full conquest was not realized until the period of the monarchy and David's military successes in the region. The text notes that no land was allotted to Levi, the priestly tribe. Since the Lord was their "heritage," they received no geographical territory (13:14). In fact, because of their unique vocation, the Levites would be found throughout the country as a whole.

14:1-15 Special considerations

Land distribution is carried out by the leaders designated by Moses: Joshua, the priest Eleazar, Aaron's son (Exod 6:25), and the tribal family heads (14:1-2; Num 32:28). This was done by lots, a customary way of determining God's will (Num 26:55-56). However, prior to distribution, two other issues are considered, both connected with distinct traditions. One explains the number twelve even though one tribe, Levi, has been excluded. The tribe of Joseph was traditionally divided in two: Ephraim and Manasseh, named for Joseph's two sons and accorded patriarchal status at the time of Jacob's death (Gen 48:5).

⁵As the LORD had commanded Moses, so the Israelites did: they apportioned the land.

Caleb's Portion. ⁶When the Judahites approached Joshua in Gilgal, the Kenizzite Caleb, son of Jephunneh, said to him: "You know the word the LORD spoke to Moses, the man of God, concerning you and concerning me in Kadesh-barnea. ⁷I was forty years old when Moses, the servant of the LORD, sent me from Kadesh-barnea to reconnoiter the land; and I brought back to him a frank report. ⁸My fellow scouts who went up with me made the people's confidence melt away, but I was completely loyal to the LORD, my God. ⁹On that occasion Moses swore this oath, 'The land where you have set foot shall become your heritage and that of your descendants forever, because you have been completely loyal to the LORD, my God.' ¹⁰Now, as he promised, the LORD has preserved me these forty-five years since the LORD spoke thus to Moses while Israel journeyed in the wilderness; and now I am eighty-five years old, ¹¹but I am still as strong today as I was the day Moses sent me forth, with no less vigor whether it be for war or for any other tasks. ¹²Now give me this mountain region which the LORD promised me that day, as you yourself heard. True, the Anakim are there, with large fortified cities, but if the LORD is with me I shall be able to dispossess them, as the LORD promised." ¹³Joshua blessed Caleb, son of Jephunneh, and gave him Hebron as his heritage. ¹⁴Therefore Hebron remains the heritage of the Kenizzite Caleb, son of Jephunneh, to the present day, because he was completely loyal to the LORD, the God of Israel. ¹⁵Hebron was formerly called Kiriath-arba, for Arba, the greatest among the Anakim. And the land had rest from war.

14:6-15 Caleb

The second etiology of the chapter centers on the Calebite clan and their unique status within the tribe of Judah. Caleb's claim to settle in the city of Hebron sprang from the scouting expedition he had made with Joshua to reconnoiter the land of Canaan at Moses' behest. He and Joshua were the only two to encourage Moses to undertake the occupation. For that reason Caleb was accorded a position of status in Israel's tradition (Num 13–14). Interestingly, he is presented as both a Judahite and a Kenizzite (14:6, 14), the latter evidently an indigenous tribe which was incorporated into Israel. This foreign origin would have been added reason to attempt to legitimate the Calebite claim to one of Judah's most important sites, the first capital of David's kingdom (2 Sam 2:1-4).

These inserted etiologies, springing from independent sources, interrupt the flow of the narrative between chapters 13 and 15; this only underscores, however, the importance in which they were held. Caleb swears to remove the enemy Anakim from his territory (14:12), even though another tradition had them eliminated earlier by Joshua (11:21).

15 **Boundaries of Judah.** [1]The lot for the tribe of Judah by their clans fell toward the boundary of Edom, the wilderness of Zin in the Negeb, in the extreme south. [2]Their southern boundary ran from the end of the Salt Sea, from the tongue of land that faces the Negeb, [3]and went southward below the pass of Akrabbim, across through Zin, up to a point south of Kadesh-barnea, across to Hezron, and up to Addar; from there, looping around Karka, [4]it crossed to Azmon and then joined the Wadi of Egypt before coming out at the sea. (This is your southern boundary.) [5]The eastern boundary was the Salt Sea as far as the mouth of the Jordan.

The northern boundary climbed northward from the tongue of the sea, toward the mouth of the Jordan, [6]up to Beth-hoglah, and ran north of Beth-arabah, up to Eben-Bohan-ben-Reuben. [7]Thence the boundary climbed to Debir, north of the Valley of Achor, in the direction of the Gilgal that faces the pass of Adummim, on the south side of the wadi; from there it crossed to the waters of En-shemesh and emerged at En-rogel. [8]Climbing again to the Valley of Ben-hinnom on the southern flank of the Jebusites (that is, Jerusalem), the boundary rose to the top of the mountain at the northern end of the Valley of Rephaim, which bounds the Valley of Hinnom on the west. [9]From the top of the mountain it ran to the fountain of waters of Nephtoah, extended to the cities of Mount Ephron, and continued to Baalah, or Kiriath-jearim. [10]From Baalah the boundary curved westward to Mount Seir and passed north of the ridge of Mount Jearim (that is, Chesalon); it descended to Beth-shemesh, and ran across to Timnah. [11]It then extended along the northern flank of Ekron, continued through Shikkeron, and across to Mount Baalah, from there to include Jabneel, before it came out at the sea. [12]The western boundary was the Great Sea and its coast. This was the complete boundary of the Judahites by their clans.

Conquest by Caleb. [13]As the LORD had commanded, Joshua gave Caleb, son of Jephunneh, a portion among the Judahites, namely, Kiriath-arba (Arba was the father of Anak), that is, Hebron. [14]And Caleb dispossessed from there the three Anakim, the descendants of Anak:

15:1-12 Boundaries of Judah

The preeminence of Judah gives it first place in presenting the geographical configuration of the tribes. Its location in the south places it near the Dead Sea touching the border of Edom and part of the Negeb desert (15:1). In the north (15:6-11) it went beyond the Dead Sea to the region north of Jerusalem. The western boundary is said to be the Mediterranean (15:12), although in Joshua's time this territory was occupied by the Philistines and would remain so into the time of the monarchy.

15:13-19 Caleb and Othniel

Once again it is etiology which accounts for the narrative. It is again stated that Hebron was allotted to the Kenizzite Caleb, who took it by conquest

Sheshai, Ahiman, and Talmai. [15]From there he marched up against the inhabitants of Debir, which was formerly called Kiriath-sepher. [16]Caleb said, "To the man who attacks Kiriath-sepher and captures it, I will give my daughter Achsah in marriage." [17]Othniel captured it, the son of Caleb's brother Kenaz; so Caleb gave him his daughter Achsah in marriage. [18]When she came to him, she induced him to ask her father for some land. Then, as she alighted from the donkey, Caleb asked her, "What do you want?" [19]She answered, "Give me a present! Since you have assigned to me land in the Negeb, give me also pools of water." So he gave her the upper and the lower pools.

Cities of Judah. [20]This is the heritage of the tribe of Judahites by their clans: [21]The cities of the tribe of the Judahites in the extreme southern district toward Edom were: Kabzeel, Eder, Jagur, [22]Kinah, Dimonah, Adadah, [23]Kedesh, Hazor, and Ithnan; [24]Ziph, Telem, Bealoth, [25]Hazor-hadattah, and Kerioth-hezron (that is, Hazor); [26]Amam, Shema, Moladah, [27]Hazar-gaddah, Heshmon, Beth-pelet, [28]Hazar-shual, Beer-sheba, and Biziothiah; [29]Baalah, Iim, Ezem, [30]Eltolad, Chesil, Hormah, [31]Ziklag, Madmannah, Sansannah, [32]Lebaoth, Shilhim, and Ain and Rimmon; a total of twenty-nine cities with their villages.

[33]In the Shephelah: Eshtaol, Zorah, Ashnah, [34]Zanoah, Engannim, Tappuah, Enam, [35]Jarmuth, Adullam, Socoh, Azekah, [36]Shaaraim, Adithaim, Gederah, and Gederothaim; fourteen cities and their villages. [37]Zenan, Hadashah, Migdal-gad, [38]Dilean, Mizpeh, Joktheel, [39]Lachish, Bozkath, Eglon, [40]Cabbon, Lahmas, Chitlish, [41]Gederoth, Beth-dagon, Naamah, and Makkedah; sixteen cities and their villages. [42]Libnah, Ether, Ashan, [43]Iphtah, Ashnah, Nezib, [44]Keilah, Achzib, and Mareshah; nine cities and their villages. [45]Ekron and its towns and villages; [46]from Ekron to the sea, all the towns that lie alongside Ashdod, and their villages; [47]Ashdod and its towns and villages; Gaza and its towns and villages, as far as the Wadi of Egypt and the coast of the Great Sea.

[48]In the mountain regions: Shamir, Jattir, Socoh, [49]Dannah, Kiriath-sannah (that is, Debir), [50]Anab, Eshtemoh, Anim, [51]Goshen, Holon, and Giloh; eleven cities and their villages. [52]Arab, Dumah, Eshan, [53]Janim, Beth-tappuah, Aphekah, [54]Humtah, Kiriath-arba (that is, Hebron), and Zior; nine cities and their villages. [55]Maon, Carmel, Ziph, Juttah, [56]Jezreel,

---

(15:13-14; 14:6-15). The presence of evidently important pools in the area is explained as the gift of Othniel, Caleb's nephew, to his wife Achsah after their marriage (15:17-19; cf. Judg 3:7-11).

15:20-61 List of cities

This is evidently an administrative list of the different jurisdictions within Judah from the time of the southern kingdom. The four major regions are the south land (15:21-32), the foothills (Shephelah) (15:33-47), the hill country (15:48-60), and the desert (15:61-62). These major regions are then

Jokdeam, Zanoah, ⁵⁷Kain, Gibbeah, and Timnah; ten cities and their villages. ⁵⁸Halhul, Beth-zur, Gedor, ⁵⁹Maarath, Beth-anoth, and Eltekon; six cities and their villages. Tekoa, Ephrathah (that is, Bethlehem), Peor, Etam, Kulom, Tatam, Zores, Karim, Gallim, Bether, and Manoko; eleven cities and their villages. ⁶⁰Kiriath-baal (that is, Kiriath-jearim) and Rabbah; two cities and their villages.

⁶¹In the wilderness: Beth-arabah, Middin, Secacah, ⁶²Nibshan, Ir-hamelah, and En-gedi; six cities and their villages. ⁶³But the Jebusites who lived in Jerusalem the Judahites could not dispossess; so the Jebusites dwell in Jerusalem beside the Judahites to the present day.

16 **The Joseph Tribes.** ¹The lot that fell to the Josephites extended from the Jordan at Jericho to the waters of Jericho east of the wilderness; then the boundary went up from Jericho to the heights at Bethel. ²Leaving Bethel for Luz, it crossed the ridge to the border of the Archites at Ataroth, ³and descended westward to the border of the Japhletites, to that of the Lower Beth-horon, and to Gezer, and from there to the sea.

Ephraim. ⁴Within the heritage of Manasseh and Ephraim, sons of Joseph, ⁵the dividing line for the heritage of the Ephraimites by their clans ran from east of Ataroth-addar to Upper Beth-horon ⁶and thence to the sea. From Michmethath on the north, their boundary curved eastward around Taanath-shiloh, and continued east of it to Janoah; ⁷from there it descended to Ataroth and Naarah, and reaching Jericho, it ended at the Jordan. ⁸From Tappuah the boundary ran westward to the Wadi Kanah and ended at the sea. This was the heritage of the Ephraimites by their clans, ⁹including the villages that belonged to each city set aside for the Ephraimites within the heritage of the Manassites. ¹⁰But they did not dispossess the Canaanites living in Gezer; they live within Ephraim to the present day, though they have been put to forced labor.

---

divided into smaller sectors, each section punctuated in the text by citing the number of cities. An interesting footnote is the continued presence of the Jebusites, from whom Jerusalem was taken by David (2 Sam 5), still maintaining a presence in the city at a much later date (15:63). The major Philistine cities, to be taken only at a later date, are also listed (15:45-47).

16:1-10 The Joseph tribes

The geographical sequence is again interrupted, with Benjamin and Dan to the north of Judah bypassed, to treat the important Joseph tribes, named for Ephraim and Manasseh, the patriarch's sons. Ephraim bordered Benjamin and Dan in the south and met Manasseh in the north at Taanahshiloh on the east and the gorge of Kanah in the west. Its eastern boundary reached the Jordan (16:7) and on the west the Mediterranean at some point (16:8). Again reference is made to a non-Israelite population present in the region (16:10).

17 **Manasseh.** ¹Now as for the lot that fell to the tribe of Manasseh as the firstborn of Joseph: since Manasseh's eldest son, Machir, the father of Gilead, was a warrior, who had already obtained Gilead and Bashan, ²the allotment was now made to the rest of the Manassites by their clans: the descendants of Abiezer, Helek, Asriel, Shechem, Hepher, and Shemida; these are the other male children of Manasseh, son of Joseph, by their clans.

³Furthermore, Zelophehad, son of Hepher, son of Gilead, son of Machir, son of Manasseh, had no sons, but only daughters, whose names were Mahlah, Noah, Hoglah, Milcah, and Tirzah. ⁴These presented themselves to Eleazar the priest, to Joshua, son of Nun, and to the leaders, saying, "The LORD commanded Moses to give us a heritage among our relatives." So in accordance with the command of the LORD a heritage was given them among their father's relatives. ⁵Thus ten shares fell to Manasseh apart from the land of Gilead and Bashan beyond the Jordan, ⁶since these female descendants of Manasseh received each a portion among his sons. The land of Gilead fell to the rest of the Manassites.

⁷Manasseh bordered on Asher. From Michmethath, near Shechem, another boundary ran southward to include the inhabitants of En-Tappuah, ⁸because the district of Tappuah belonged to Manasseh, although Tappuah itself was an Ephraimite city on the border of Manasseh. ⁹This same boundary continued down to the Wadi Kanah. The cities that belonged to Ephraim from among the cities in Manasseh were those to the south of that wadi; thus the territory of Manasseh ran north of the wadi and ended at the sea. ¹⁰The land on the south belonged to Ephraim and that on the north to Manasseh; with the sea as their common boundary, they reached Asher on the north and Issachar on the east. ¹¹Moreover, in Issachar and in Asher Manasseh was awarded Beth-shean and

17:1-18 More on Joseph

The chapter deals with added issues concerning Manasseh and Ephraim, including Manasseh's allocation west of the Jordan (17:1-10), the continued presence of Canaanites within the territory (17:11-13), and the tribes' request for more territory (17:14-18).

17:1-10

The western territory of Manasseh lay between Issachar on the north and Ephraim on the south. Its western boundary was the Mediterranean coast, and, despite verse 7, it touched on Asher at one coastal point only. Its location in central Palestine later became the hub of Samaria. The tribal land was divided among twelve clans: two in Transjordan and ten west of the Jordan, with five of the latter identified with women, the daughters of one Zelophehad (17:1-6).

its towns, Ibleam and its towns, the inhabitants of Dor and its towns, the inhabitants of Endor and its towns, the inhabitants of Taanach and its towns, the inhabitants of Megiddo and its towns (the third is Naphath-dor). ¹²Since the Manassites were not able to dispossess these cities, the Canaanites continued to inhabit this region. ¹³When the Israelites grew stronger they put the Canaanites to forced labor, but they did not dispossess them.

Protest of Joseph Tribes. ¹⁴The descendants of Joseph said to Joshua, "Why have you given us only one lot and one share as our heritage? Our people are too many, because of the extent to which the LORD has blessed us." ¹⁵Joshua answered them, "If you are too many, go up to the forest and clear out a place for yourselves there in the land of the Perizzites and Rephaim, since the mountain regions of Ephraim are so narrow." ¹⁶For the Josephites said, "Our mountain regions are not enough for us; on the other hand, the Canaanites living in the valley region all have iron chariots, in particular those in Beth-shean and its towns, and those in the valley of Jezreel." ¹⁷Joshua therefore said to Ephraim and Manasseh, the house of Joseph, "You are a numerous people and very strong. You shall not have merely one share, ¹⁸for the mountain region which is now forest shall be yours when you clear it. Its adjacent land shall also be yours if, despite their strength and iron chariots, you dispossess the Canaanites."

18 ¹The whole community of the Israelites assembled at Shiloh, where they set up the tent of meeting; and the land was subdued before them.

The Seven Remaining Portions. ²There remained seven tribes among the

17:11-13

The cities which remained unconquered and occupied by Canaanites correspond to those cited elsewhere (Judg 1:27). While located in the territory of Manasseh, they were evidently identified as well with Asher and Issachar as border cities in the Jezreel valley. The author attempts to reconcile the two viewpoints with an oblique reference to the two tribes (17:11).

17:14-18

Two traditions are reflected in Joseph's request for more land. In the first Joshua responds to the request by urging them to clear the forest and settle in the land already designated (17:14-15). The second deals with the threat of the Canaanites in the region with their formidable military prowess in the Josephite territory (17:16), with Joshua again urging continued expansion (17:17-18). The reference to iron chariots (17:16) recalls the earlier introduction of the chariot in Near Eastern warfare by the Hyksos (17:16).

18:1–19:51 Land distribution to the seven remaining tribes

There is a time lapse here to allow for the subduing of hostile forces and surveying the territory (18:1-10). From another point of view, it provides

Israelites that had not yet received their heritage. ³Joshua therefore said to the Israelites, "How much longer will you put off taking steps to possess the land which the LORD, the God of your ancestors, has given you? ⁴Choose three representatives from each of your tribes; I will send them to go throughout the land and describe it for purposes of acquiring their heritage. When they return to me ⁵you shall divide it into seven parts. Judah is to retain its territory in the south, and the house of Joseph its territory in the north. ⁶You shall bring to me here the description of the land in seven sections. I will then cast lots for you here before the LORD, our God. ⁷For the Levites have no share among you, because the priesthood of the LORD is their heritage; while Gad, Reuben, and the half-tribe of Manasseh have already received the heritage east of the Jordan which Moses, the servant of the LORD, gave them."

⁸When those who were to describe the land were ready for their journey, Joshua commanded them, "Go throughout the land and describe it; return to me and I will cast lots for you here before the LORD in Shiloh." ⁹So they went through the land, described its cities in writing in seven sections, and returned to Joshua in the camp at Shiloh. ¹⁰Joshua then cast lots for them before the LORD in Shiloh, and divided up the land for the Israelites into their separate shares.

Benjamin. ¹¹One lot fell to the tribe of Benjaminites by their clans. The territory allotted them lay between the

---

sufficient separation from the allotment given to the major tribes, Judah and Joseph, before turning to the less important tribes: Benjamin (18:11-28), Simeon (19:1-9), Zebulun (19:10-16), Issachar (19:17-23), Asher (19:24-31), Naphtali (19:32-39), and Dan (19:40-48).

18:1-10

The action is now situated in Shiloh, an important sanctuary in later times, identified with the prophet Samuel. The mention of the meeting tent is unusual in the Deuteronomistic tradition. It was a vital part of the religious experience during the desert sojourn and is prominent in the priestly (P) tradition. It may show the influence of priestly sources in the final text.

Land assignment is judiciously and cautiously executed. Scouts from each tribe are to survey the land; the cities are listed in seven sections. With fair distribution among the seven, Joshua then cast lots to determine the Lord's will for each tribe (18:4-7). Excluded from consideration were Judah, Reuben, Gad, and Manasseh, already determined, and Levi, the priestly tribe (18:5-7).

18:11-28

The relatively small but politically important territory allotted to Benjamin lay between Ephraim in the north and Judah in the south. It was bound by the Jordan (east), the region of Jericho and Bethel (north), by

descendants of Judah and those of Joseph. ¹²Their northern boundary began at the Jordan and went over the northern flank of Jericho, up westward into the mountains, until it reached the wilderness of Beth-aven. ¹³From there it crossed over to the southern flank of Luz (that is, Bethel). Then it ran down to Ataroth-addar, on the mountaintop south of Lower Beth-horon. ¹⁴For the western border, the boundary line swung south from the mountaintop opposite Beth-horon until it reached Kiriath-baal (that is, Kiriath-jearim; this city belonged to the Judahites). This was the western boundary. ¹⁵The southern boundary began at the limits of Kiriath-jearim and projected to the spring at Nephtoah. ¹⁶It went down to the edge of the mountain on the north of the Valley of Rephaim, where it faces the Valley of Ben-hinnom; and continuing down the Valley of Hinnom along the southern flank of the Jebusites, reached En-rogel. ¹⁷Inclining to the north, it extended to En-shemesh, and thence to Geliloth, opposite the pass of Adummim. Then it dropped to Eben-Bohan-ben-Reuben, ¹⁸across the northern flank of the Arabah overlook, down into the Arabah. ¹⁹From there the boundary continued across the northern flank of Beth-hoglah and extended northward to the tongue of the Salt Sea, toward the southern end of the Jordan. This was the southern boundary. ²⁰The Jordan bounded it on the east. This was how the heritage of the Benjaminites by their clans was bounded on all sides.

²¹Now the cities belonging to the tribe of the Benjaminites by their clans were: Jericho, Beth-hoglah, Emek-keziz, ²²Beth-arabah, Zemaraim, Bethel, ²³Avvim, Parah, Ophra, ²⁴Chephar-ammoni, Ophni, and Geba; twelve cities and their villages. ²⁵Also Gibeon, Ramah, Beeroth, ²⁶Mizpeh, Chephirah, Mozah, ²⁷Rekem, Irpeel, Taralah, ²⁸Zela, Haeleph, the Jebusite city (that is, Jerusalem), Gibeah, and Kiriath; fourteen cities and their villages. This was the heritage of the clans of Benjaminites.

Kireath-jearim (west). On the south its boundaries with Judah correspond to those already cited (15:6-11).

The list of cities (18:21-28) was evidently one of the administrative sub-divisions mentioned earlier in connection with Judah (15:20-63), pointing to a period in which the boundaries between the two tribes were more fluid. Here the list includes important cities such as Jericho and Bethel. There is reference to the "Jebusite city (that is, Jerusalem)" (18:28). The city was probably unidentified originally, since Jerusalem would hardly be listed as Benjaminite or Judahite on an administrative list. Moreover, the importance of its being conquered by David would hardly permit a reference to it as a Jebusite city. That Jebusites remained in the region, however, is entirely likely.

In chapter 19, portions are allotted to the remaining tribes. For clarity the reader is referred to a map indicating the location of the tribes throughout the land. Here we shall paint with a broad brush, limiting our comments to the more salient features.

19 **Simeon.** [1]The second lot fell to Simeon. The heritage of the tribe of Simeonites by their clans lay within that of the Judahites. [2]For their heritage they received Beer-sheba, Shema, Moladah, [3]Hazar-shual, Balah, Ezem, [4]Eltolad, Bethul, Hormah, [5]Ziklag, Bethmar-caboth, Hazar-susah, [6]Beth-lebaoth, and Sharuhen; thirteen cities and their villages. [7]Also Ain, Rimmon, Ether, and Ashan; four cities and their villages, [8]besides all the villages around these cities as far as Baalath-beer (that is, Ramoth-negeb). This was the heritage of the tribe of the Simeonites by their clans. [9]This heritage of the Simeonites was within the confines of the Judahites; for since the portion of the latter was too large for them, the Simeonites obtained their heritage within it.

Zebulun. [10]The third lot fell to the Zebulunites by their clans. The boundary of their heritage was at Sarid. [11]Their boundary went up west and through Mareal, reaching Dabbesheth and the wadi that is near Jokneam. [12]From Sarid eastward it ran to the district of Chisloth-tabor, on to Daberath, and up to Japhia. [13]From there it continued eastward to Gath-hepher and to Eth-kazin, extended to Rimmon, and turned to Neah. [14]Skirting north of Hannathon, the boundary ended at the valley of Iphtahel. [15]Thus, with Kattath, Nahalal, Shimron, Idalah, and Bethlehem, there were twelve cities and their villages. [16]This was the heritage of the Zebulunites by their clans, these cities and their villages.

Issachar. [17]The fourth lot fell to Issachar. The territory of the Issacharites by their clans [18]included Jezreel, Chesulloth, Shunem, [19]Hapharaim, Shion, Anaharath, [20]Rabbith, Kishion, Ebez, [21]Remeth, En-gannim, En-haddah, and Beth-pazzez. [22]The boundary reached Tabor, Shahazumah, and Beth-shemesh, ending at the Jordan: sixteen cities and their

---

Simeon

(19:1-10) seems to have lost its original identity, if indeed it ever had one, in being entirely absorbed in the larger tribe of Judah. It is a relationship alluded to in the present text (19:1, 9). No geographical boundaries are noted; most of the cities cited are already found on the Judah list (15:20-63). This section may well be a Deuteronomistic construct of a tribe which no longer enjoyed an independent existence.

Zebulun

(19:10-16) occupied the Plain of Esdraelon in the lower hills of Galilee. Moving clockwise, it was bounded by Naphtali, Issachar, Manasseh, and Asher. A small northern tribe, it claimed twelve cities and their villages.

Issachar

(19:17-23), another northern tribe, was also located on the Plain of Esdraelon. Bounded on the east by the Jordan and the southern end of the Lake of Galilee, it reached Naphtali in the north, Manasseh in the south, and Zebulun and Manasseh in the west.

villages. ²³This was the heritage of the Issacharites by their clans, these cities and their villages.

Asher. ²⁴The fifth lot fell to the Asherites by their clans. ²⁵Their territory included Helkath, Hali, Beten, Achshaph, ²⁶Allammelech, Amad, and Mishal, and reached Carmel on the west, and Shihor-libnath. ²⁷In the other direction, it ran eastward of Beth-dagon, reached Zebulun and the valley of Iphtahel; then north of Beth-emek and Neiel, it extended northward to Cabul, ²⁸Ebron, Rehob, Hammon, and Kanah, near Greater Sidon. ²⁹Then the boundary turned back to Ramah and to the fortress city of Tyre; thence it cut back to Hosah and ended at the sea. Thus, with Mahalab, Achzib, ³⁰Ummah, Acco, Aphek, and Rehob, there were twenty-two cities and their villages. ³¹This was the heritage of the tribe of the Asherites by their clans, these cities and their villages.

Naphtali. ³²The sixth lot fell to the Naphtalites. ³³Their boundary extended from Heleph, from the oak at Zaananim, including Adami-nekeb and Jabneel, to Lakkum, and ended at the Jordan. ³⁴In the opposite direction, westerly, it ran through Aznoth-tabor and from there extended to Hukkok; it reached Zebulun on the south, Asher on the west, and the Jordan on the east. ³⁵The fortified cities were Ziddim, Zer, Hammath, Rakkath, Chinnereth, ³⁶Adamah, Ramah, Hazor, ³⁷Kedesh, Edrei, En-hazor, ³⁸Yiron, Migdal-el, Horem, Beth-anath, and Beth-shemesh; nineteen cities and their villages. ³⁹This was the heritage of the tribe of the Naphtalites by their clans, these cities and their villages.

Dan. ⁴⁰The seventh lot fell to the tribe of Danites by their clans. ⁴¹Their heritage was the territory of Zorah, Eshtaol, Irshemesh, ⁴²Shaalabbin, Aijalon, Ithlah, ⁴³Elon, Timnah, Ekron, ⁴⁴Eltekoh, Gibbethon, Baalath, ⁴⁵Jehud, Bene-berak, Gath-rimmon, ⁴⁶Me-jarkon, and Rakkon, with the coast at Joppa. ⁴⁷But the territory of the Danites was too small for them; so the Danites marched up and

Asher

(19:24-31), one of the northernmost tribes, went as far as the boundary of Phoenicia. A large territory, it extended as far as the Carmel mountains in the south. It was contiguous with Zebulun and Manasseh.

Naphtali

(19:32-39) parallels Asher in the northeast. Geographically it extended from the Jordan valley in the south to Lake Huleh, above the Sea of Galilee, in the north. On its west and south it touched on Asher, Zebulun, and Issachar.

And finally the tribe of Dan

(19:40-48) was originally assigned a small portion of land in the region of Judah and Ephraim. Oppressed by the Amorites, they could not appropriate their land (Judg 1:34-35). Their further oppression is recounted

attacked Leshem, which they captured and put to the sword. Once they had taken possession of Leshem, they dwelt there and named it after their ancestor Dan. ⁴⁸This was the heritage of the tribe of the Danites by their clans, these cities and their villages.

Joshua's City. ⁴⁹When the last of them had received the portions of the land they were to inherit, the Israelites assigned a heritage in their midst to Joshua, son of Nun. ⁵⁰According to the command of the LORD, they gave him the city he requested, Timnah-serah in the mountain region of Ephraim. He rebuilt the city and made it his home.

⁵¹These are the heritages which Eleazar the priest, Joshua, son of Nun, and the heads of families in the tribes of the Israelites apportioned by lot in the presence of the LORD, at the door of the tent of meeting in Shiloh. Thus they finished dividing the land.

20 **Cities of Refuge.** ¹ The LORD said to Joshua: ²Tell the Israelites: Designate for yourselves the cities of refuge of which I spoke to you through Moses, ³to which anyone guilty of inadvertent and unintentional homicide may flee for asylum from the avenger of blood. ⁴To one of these cities the killer shall flee, and standing at the entrance of the city gate, shall plead his case in the hearing of the elders of the city, who must receive him and assign him a place in which to live among them. ⁵Though the avenger of blood pursues him, they shall not deliver up to him the one who killed a neighbor unintentionally, when there had been no hatred previously. ⁶Once he has stood judgment before the community, he shall live on in that city until the death of the high priest who is in office at the time. Then the killer may return home to the city from where he originally fled.

List of Cities. ⁷So they set apart Kedesh in Galilee in the mountain region of Naphtali, Shechem in the mountain region of Ephraim, and Kiriath-arba (that is, Hebron) in the mountain region

---

in the Samson story (Judg 13–16). The tribe finally moved north. Their conquest of Leshem (Laish; 19:47) is recounted in Judges (ch. 18). This was the northernmost tribe, reaching the Valley of Lebanon and Mt. Hermon.

As his personal inheritance, Joshua received the city of Timnah-serah in Ephraim which he restored as his personal home. It may be identified with the later Khirbet Tibneh in the central region of Shechem (19:49-50).

20:1-9 Cities of refuge

The recompense for serious sin moved toward the guilty person with an almost physical sense of inexorability. This was the "boomerang" quality of sin as the ancients envisioned it. In the case of homicide, the avenging agent was the next of kin with the act to be executed as soon as possible (Gen 9:6). Far from being sinful, such revenge was a moral imperative. Hence, provision had to be made in the case of accidental killing. Mosaic legislation (Num 35:9-28), spoken of here (20:1-2) provided for cities to

of Judah. ⁸And beyond the Jordan east of Jericho they designated Bezer in the wilderness on the tableland in the tribe of Reuben, Ramoth in Gilead in the tribe of Gad, and Golan in Bashan in the tribe of Manasseh. ⁹These are the designated cities to which any Israelite or alien residing among them who had killed a person unintentionally might flee to escape death at the hand of the avenger of blood, until the killer could appear before the community.

21 **Levitical Cities.** ¹The heads of the Levite families approached Eleazar the priest, Joshua, son of Nun, and the heads of families of the other tribes of the Israelites ²at Shiloh in the land of Canaan, and said to them, "The LORD commanded, through Moses, that cities be given us to dwell in, with pasture lands for our livestock." ³Out of their own heritage, according to the command of the LORD, the Israelites gave the Levites the following cities with their pasture lands.

⁴When the first lot among the Levites fell to the clans of the Kohathites, the descendants of Aaron the priest obtained by lot from the tribes of Judah, Simeon, and Benjamin, thirteen cities. ⁵From the clans of the tribe of Ephraim, from the tribe of Dan, and from the half-tribe of Manasseh, the rest of the Kohathites obtained by lot ten cities. ⁶From the clans of the tribe of Issachar, from the tribe of Asher, from the tribe of Naphtali, and from the half-tribe of Manasseh, the Gershonites obtained by lot thirteen cities. ⁷From the tribes of Reuben, Gad, and Zebulun, the clans of the Merarites obtained twelve cities. ⁸These cities with their pasture lands the Israelites gave by

---

which the offender could flee and be safe from harm until his case could be adjudicated (20:6). If he was proved innocent he could remain safe within the city. Judgment was passed by the elders (20:4). An awkward attempt to include other legislation accounts for the mention of community judgment as well (20:6). The death of the main priest in the community left the person free to leave.

Needless to say, these cities had to be readily accessible. Distance could mean death at the hands of the avenger. Conveniently, three were located east and three west of the Jordan (20:7-9).

21:1-45 The Levitical cities

The often repeated injunction that no land allotment was to be given to the tribe of Levi left the question of their future provision unresolved. Thus this final chapter on land distribution treats exclusively of the Levites. They were to be given a number of cities throughout the country with surrounding pastureland to serve as a home for them and locations where priestly service could be offered to the people. This was done in accord with the Mosaic directive (Num 35:1-8). This did not mean that Levites alone occupied these cities; they were situated among the tribes whose citizens lived

lot to the Levites, as the LORD had commanded through Moses.

Cities of the Priests. [9] From the tribes of the Judahites and Simeonites they gave the following cities [10] and assigned them to the descendants of Aaron in the Kohathite clan of the Levites, since the first lot fell to them: [11] first, Kiriath-arba (Arba was the father of Anak), that is, Hebron, in the mountain region of Judah, with the adjacent pasture lands, [12] although the open country and villages belonging to the city had been given to Caleb, son of Jephunneh, as his holding. [13] Thus to the descendants of Aaron the priest were given the city of refuge for homicides at Hebron, with its pasture lands; also, Libnah with its pasture lands, [14] Jattir with its pasture lands, Eshtemoa with its pasture lands, [15] Holon with its pasture lands, Debir with its pasture lands, [16] Ain with its pasture lands, Juttah with its pasture lands, and Beth-shemesh with its pasture lands: nine cities from these two tribes. [17] From the tribe of Benjamin they obtained Gibeon with its pasture lands, Geba with its pasture lands, [18] Anathoth with its pasture lands, and Almon with its pasture lands: four cities. [19] These cities which with their pasture lands belonged to the priestly descendants of Aaron, were thirteen in all.

Cities of the Other Kohathites. [20] The rest of the Kohathite clans among the Levites obtained by lot, from the tribe of Ephraim, four cities. [21] They were assigned, with its pasture lands, the city of refuge for homicides at Shechem in the mountain region of Ephraim; also Gezer with its pasture lands, [22] Kibzaim with its pasture lands, and Beth-horon with its pasture lands. [23] From the tribe of Dan they obtained Elteke with its pasture lands, Gibbethon with its pasture lands, [24] Aijalon with its pasture lands, and Gath-rimmon with its pasture lands: four cities. [25] From the half-tribe of Manasseh, Taanach with its pasture lands, and Gath-rimmon with its pasture lands: two cities. [26] These cities which with their pasture lands belonged to the rest of the Kohathite clans were ten in all.

Cities of the Gershonites. [27] The Gershonite clan of the Levites received from the half-tribe of Manasseh the city of refuge for homicides at Golan in Bashan, with its pasture lands; and also Beth-Astharoth with its pasture lands: two cities. [28] From the tribe of Issachar they obtained Kishion with its pasture lands, Daberath with its pasture lands,

---

there as well, as would be seen clearly in the case of places like Hebron, Shechem, and Ramath-gilead.

Some authors argue that the list is artificial, with its neat division of four cities for each tribe in a territory which in early times would have been very vast. All of this points to the fact, it is said, that the list lacks historical accuracy. On the other hand, some see considerable historical possibility, especially in light of the expansion that took place during David's reign, which could see the cities as placed within a royal administrative territory. In addition, the rather clumsy clustering of the cities is hardly consonant

²⁹Jarmuth with its pasture lands, and Engannim with its pasture lands: four cities. ³⁰From the tribe of Asher, Mishal with its pasture lands, Abdon with its pasture lands, ³¹Helkath with its pasture lands, and Rehob with its pasture lands: four cities. ³²From the tribe of Naphtali, the city of refuge for homicides at Kedesh in Galilee, with its pasture lands; also Hammath with its pasture lands, and Kartan with its pasture lands: three cities. ³³The cities which belonged to the Gershonite clans, with their pasture lands, were thirteen in all.

Cities of the Merarites. ³⁴The Merarite clans, the last of the Levites, received, from the tribe of Zebulun, Jokneam with its pasture lands, Kartah with its pasture lands, ³⁵Dimnah with its pasture lands, and Nahalal with its pasture lands: four cities. ³⁶Also, across the Jordan, from the tribe of Reuben, the city of refuge for homicides at Bezer with its pasture lands, Jahaz with its pasture lands, ³⁷Kedemoth with its pasture lands, and Mephaath with its pasture lands:

four cities. ³⁸From the tribe of Gad, the city of refuge for homicides at Ramoth in Gilead with its pasture lands, Mahanaim with its pasture lands, ³⁹Heshbon with its pasture lands, and Jazer with its pasture lands: four cities in all. ⁴⁰The cities allotted to the Merarite clans, the last of the Levites, were therefore twelve in all.

⁴¹Thus the total number of cities within the territory of the Israelites which, with their pasture lands, belonged to the Levites, was forty-eight. ⁴²With each and every one of these cities went the pasture lands round about it.

⁴³And so the LORD gave Israel the entire land he had sworn to their ancestors he would give them. Once they had taken possession of it, and dwelt in it, ⁴⁴the LORD gave them peace on every side, just as he had promised their ancestors. Not one of their enemies could withstand them; the LORD gave all their enemies into their power. ⁴⁵Not a single word of the blessing that the LORD had promised to the house of Israel failed; it all came true.

---

with a neat idealized list. In view of the administrative as well as cultic role of the priests, the Levitical cities make considerable administrative sense, especially in the far flung regions of the country.

The descendants of Levi, in an admittedly artificial setting, are listed under three headings: Kohathites (12:3-5), Gershonites (21:6), and the Merarites (21:7). Highlighted as a group are the descendants of Aaron (Kohathites), who receive thirteen cities in Judah, Simeon, and Benjamin (21:4), with ten given to the remaining Kohathites (21:5); thirteen to the Gershonites (21:6); and twelve to the Merarites (21:7). The total number of Levitical cities was forty-eight. Four cities were allotted to each tribe, with the exception of Judah/Simeon (nine) and Naphtali (three). The list includes all of the cities of refuge (ch. 20) where the priestly presence was particularly important.

III. Return of the Transjordan Tribes and Joshua's Farewell

22 **The Eastern Tribes Dismissed.** ¹At that time Joshua summoned the Reubenites, the Gadites, and the half-tribe of Manasseh ²and said to them: "You have observed all that Moses, the servant of the LORD, commanded you, and have listened to my voice in everything I commanded you. ³For many years now, even until today, you have not abandoned your allies, but have taken care to observe the commands of the LORD, your God. ⁴Now that the LORD, your God, has settled your allies as he promised them, you may return to your tents, to your own land, which Moses, the servant of the LORD, gave you, across

---

APPENDIX

Joshua 22–24

22:1-34 Problems in Transjordan

The story is clear enough in its broad outline. The two and one-half tribes given land east of the Jordan were sent back to their homeland by Joshua. Once there they constructed an altar which was seen as a secessionist gesture and cultically objectionable as opposed to the single sanctuary within Canaan proper. Before military action was taken, a delegation was sent to investigate the matter, only to be reassured that the altar was not for sacrifice but rather a symbol of unity. The delegation returned and reported their favorable findings to Joshua and the Israelites.

Two underlying motifs important to the Deuteronomist are significant in the narrative. The first lies in the preeminence accorded Canaan itself, "the land the LORD possesses" (22:19). The repeated efforts to legitimate the Transjordanian tribes in the biblical narrative is a clear indication of their secondary, even controversial status. In fact there were moments when they were opponents of Israel proper (Judg 12:1-6). The second motif underscores the later centralization of all cult in Israel under king Josiah in the seventh century. Jerusalem alone was the place of worship, and all other places of cult were destroyed (2 Kgs 22–23). This was a reform particularly close to the Deuteronomist, who gives this centralization repeated emphasis.

22:1-9 The commission of the tribes

The legitimacy of the claim of the Transjordanian tribes as being true Israelites is highlighted in Joshua's statement, as they are exhorted to continued fidelity in strongly Deuteronomistic language (22:1-6). They return home with a more than sufficient share of the booty from the conquest (22:7-9).

the Jordan. [5]But be very careful to observe the commandment and the law which Moses, the servant of the LORD, commanded you: love the LORD, your God, follow him in all his ways, keep his commandments, hold fast to him, and serve him with your whole heart and your whole self." [6]Joshua then blessed them and sent them away, and they went to their tents.

[7](For, to half of the tribe of Manasseh Moses had assigned land in Bashan; and to the other half Joshua had given a portion along with their allies west of the Jordan.) When Joshua sent them away to their tents and blessed them, [8]he said, "Now that you are returning to your own tents with great wealth, with abundant livestock, with silver, gold, bronze and iron, and with a very large supply of clothing, divide these spoils of your enemies with your allies there." [9]So the Reubenites, the Gadites, and the half-tribe of Manasseh left the other Israelites at Shiloh in the land of Canaan and returned to the land of Gilead, their own land, which they had received according to the LORD's command through Moses.

The Altar Beside the Jordan. [10]When the Reubenites, the Gadites, and the half-tribe of Manasseh came to the region of the Jordan in the land of Canaan, they built an altar there at the Jordan, an impressively large altar. [11]The other Israelites heard the report: "The Reubenites, the Gadites, and the half-tribe of Manasseh have built an altar" in the region of the Jordan facing the land of Canaan, across from the Israelites. [12]When the Israelites heard this, they assembled at Shiloh, as the entire Israelite community to take military action against them.

Accusation of the Western Tribes. [13]The Israelites sent Phinehas, son of Eleazar the priest, to the Reubenites, the Gadites, and the half-tribe of Manasseh in the land of Gilead, [14]and with him ten leaders, one from each tribe of Israel, each one the head of an ancestral house among the clans of Israel. [15]When these came to the Reubenites, the Gadites, and the half-tribe of Manasseh in the land of Gilead, they said to them: [16]"Thus says the whole community of the LORD: What act of treachery is this you have committed

22:10-20 The construction of the altar

From the initial mention it is not clear on which side of the Jordan the altar was built (22:10). but it is quickly clarified as being in Transjordan (v.11). The act was seen as immediately provocative in compromising the singular character of the sanctuary at Shiloh, and a call to arms was issued (22:10-11; cf. 18:1). The diplomatic embassy consisted of the priest Phinehas and one prince from each tribe west of the Jordan (22:13-14). The accusation was of serious cultic violation and possible secessionist intent. The action of the Transjordanians was compared to the idolatry of the Baal of Peor in the desert where illicit cultic sex and other pagan rites had prevailed (Num 25). The present action was seen as having collective consequences as in the case of Achan (7:20). The people were advised that if they saw their land as unclean, they always had the right to cross the Jordan and worship there.

against the God of Israel? This day you have turned from following the LORD; by building an altar of your own you have rebelled against the LORD this day. ¹⁷Is the iniquity of Peor not enough, by which we made ourselves impure, even to this day, and a plague came upon the community of the LORD? ¹⁸If today you turn away from following the LORD, and rebel against the LORD, tomorrow he will be angry with the whole community of Israel! ¹⁹If you consider the land you now possess unclean, cross over to the land the LORD possesses, where the tabernacle of the LORD stands, and share that with us. But do not rebel against the LORD, nor involve us in rebellion, by building an altar of your own in addition to the altar of the LORD, our God. ²⁰When Achan, son of Zerah, acted treacherously by violating the ban, was it not upon the entire community of Israel that wrath fell? Though he was but a single man, he did not perish alone for his guilt!"

Reply of the Eastern Tribes. ²¹The Reubenites, the Gadites, and the half-tribe of Manasseh replied to the heads of the Israelite clans: ²²"The LORD is the God of gods. The LORD, the God of gods, knows and Israel shall know. If now we have acted out of rebellion or treachery against the LORD, our God, do not try to save us this day, ²³and if we have built an altar of our own to turn from following the LORD, or to sacrifice burnt offerings, grain offer-

ings, or communion sacrifices upon it, the LORD himself will exact the penalty. ²⁴We did it rather out of our anxious concern lest in the future your children should say to our children: 'What have you to do with the LORD, the God of Israel? ²⁵For the LORD has placed the Jordan as a boundary between you and us, you Reubenites and Gadites. You have no share in the LORD.' Thus your children would prevent ours from revering the LORD. ²⁶So we thought, 'Let us act for ourselves by building this altar of our own'—not for burnt offerings or sacrifice, ²⁷but as witness between us and you and our descendants, that we have the right to provide for the service of the LORD in his presence with our burnt offerings, sacrifices, and communion sacrifices. Now in the future your children cannot say to our children, 'You have no share in the LORD.' ²⁸Our thought was that, if in the future they should speak thus to us or to our descendants, we could answer: 'Look at the copy of the altar of the LORD which our ancestors made, not for burnt offerings or for sacrifices, but to witness between you and us.' ²⁹Far be it from us to rebel against the LORD or to turn now from following the LORD by building an altar for burnt offering, grain offering, or sacrifice in addition to the altar of the LORD, our God, which stands before his tabernacle."

³⁰When Phinehas the priest and the leaders of the community, the heads of

22:21-31 The response

The episode ends on a positive note, with the presence of the altar taking on etiological importance (22:34). It was intended as a symbol of unity, not a place of sacrifice (22:21-29). It was not to compete with Shiloh where the Tent of the Lord's Dwelling was located. Rather it was to be a "witness" to the Israelite clans, heard what the Reubenites, the Gadites, and the Manassites had to say, they were satisfied. ³¹Phinehas, son of Eleazar the priest, said to the Reubenites, the Gadites, and the Manassites, "Today we know that the LORD is in our midst. Since you have not rebelled against the LORD by this act of treachery, you have delivered the Israelites from the hand of the LORD."

³²Phinehas, son of Eleazar the priest, and the leaders returned from the Reubenites and the Gadites in the land of Gilead to the Israelites in the land of Canaan, and reported the matter to them. ³³The report satisfied the Israelites, who blessed God and decided not to take military action against the Reubenites and Gadites nor to ravage the land where they lived.

³⁴The Reubenites and the Gadites gave the altar its name as a witness among them that the LORD is God.

23 **Joshua's Final Plea.** ¹Many years later, after the LORD had given the Israelites rest from all their enemies round about them, and when Joshua was old and advanced in years, ²he summoned all Israel, including their elders, leaders, judges and officers, and said to them: "I am old and advanced in years. ³You have seen all that the LORD, your God, has done for you against all these nations; for it has been the LORD, your God, who fought for you. ⁴See, I have apportioned among your tribes as their heritage the nations that survive, as well as those I destroyed, between the Jordan and the Great Sea in the west. ⁵The LORD, your God, will drive them out and dispossess them at your approach, so that you will take possession of their land as the LORD, your God, promised you. ⁶Therefore be strong and be careful to observe all that is written in the book of the law of Moses, never turning from it right or left, ⁷or mingling with these nations that survive among you. You must not invoke their gods by name, or swear by them, or serve them, or bow down to them, ⁸but you must hold fast to the LORD, your God, as you have done up

the exclusive worship of YHWH in the duly designated sanctuary, as well as to the unity of all the tribes. The name "witness" was given to the altar (22:34), and peace was restored within all of Israel.

23:1-24 Final exhortation

The chapter is Deuteronomistic in content and style. Its strong parallelism with chapter 24 may point to the incorporation of two distinct documents. It is certain that the present chapter has been reworked and edited by the Deuteronomist. The next chapter is located in Shechem; the present one is presumably in Shiloh. The parallels between Joshua and Moses have been mentioned earlier in the commentary. Here again it appears between Moses' farewell address (Deut 32–33) and the present discourse. The passage also bears similarity with the final words of David to his son Solomon (1 Kgs 2:1-10).

to this day. ⁹At your approach the LORD has dispossessed great and strong nations; not one has withstood you up to this day. ¹⁰One of you puts to flight a thousand, because it is the LORD, your God, himself who fights for you, as he promised you. ¹¹As for you, take great care to love the LORD, your God. ¹²For if you ever turn away from him and join with the remnant of these nations that survive among you, by intermarrying and intermingling with them, ¹³know for certain that the LORD, your God, will no longer dispossess these nations at your approach. Instead they will be a snare and a trap for you, a scourge for your sides and thorns for your eyes, until you perish from this good land which the LORD, your God, has given you.

¹⁴"Today, as you see, I am going the way of all the earth. So now acknowledge with your whole heart and soul that not one of all the promises the LORD, your God, made concerning you has failed. Every one has come true for you; not one has failed. ¹⁵But just as every promise the LORD, your God, made to you has come true for you, so will he bring upon you every threat, even so far as to exterminate you from this good land which the LORD, your God, has given you. ¹⁶If you transgress the covenant of the LORD, your God, which he enjoined on you, to go and serve other

---

The literary form, common to many ancient treaties and documents, contains a recall of past benefits and assurance for the future (23:3-5), an exhortation to fidelity (23:6-13), and a conclusion (23:14-16). In reviewing past benefits, Joshua speaks of the invasion and occupation of the land and the tribal allotments. But there is clear indication that some foreign elements still remain to be dislodged (23:4-5). The land of Canaan from the Jordan to the Mediterranean is the unmerited, wholly gratuitous heritage of Israel. It is the Lord who has led the way, fought the battles, and vanquished the foe. This recounting is intended to elicit sentiments of gratitude in the people's hearts.

For their part, the Israelites must adhere to the laws and statutes which YHWH has given. Apostasy is the great sin and it appears repeatedly in the final exhortation. Categorically excluded is any form of homage to foreign deities, as well as any form of inclusive contact or inter-marriage (23:7-8, 12).

As in Deuteronomy 27, there are threats as well as blessings. If the love of God and the observance of his laws are abandoned, the pagan countries that remain will be a continuous source of enmity and hostility (23:13). If necessary, this will lead to Israel being overcome and dislodged from the land of its inheritance.

In reading this final exhortation, there is the mounting realization that, regardless of the literary setting, the historical moment is that of the Babylonian exile of the sixth century. It was Israel's continued infidelity that led to the destruction and deportation of 586. What appears as a future

gods and bow down to them, the anger of the LORD will flare up against you and you will quickly perish from the good land he has given you."

24 **Covenant Ceremony.** ¹Joshua gathered together all the tribes of Israel at Shechem, summoning the elders, leaders, judges, and officers of Israel. When they stood in ranks before God, ²Joshua addressed all the people: "Thus says the LORD, the God of Israel: In times past your ancestors, down to Terah, father of Abraham and Nahor, lived beyond the River and served other gods. ³But I brought your father Abraham from the region beyond the River and led him through the entire land of Canaan. I made his descendants numerous, and gave him Isaac. ⁴To Isaac I gave Jacob and Esau. To Esau I assigned the mountain region of Seir to possess, while Jacob and his children went down to Egypt.

⁵"Then I sent Moses and Aaron, and struck Egypt with the plagues and wonders that I wrought in her midst. Afterward I led you out. ⁶And when I led your ancestors out of Egypt, you came to the sea, and the Egyptians pursued your ancestors to the Red Sea with chariots and charioteers. ⁷When they cried out to the LORD, he put darkness between you and the Egyptians, upon whom he brought the sea so that it covered them. Your eyes saw what I did to Egypt. After you dwelt a long time in the wilderness, ⁸I brought you into the land of the Amorites who lived east of the Jordan. They fought against you, but I

---

warning in the text recalls the sad reality of Israel's history at the time the text was written.

24:1-33 Conclusion

This celebrated chapter recounts the renewal of the covenant (24:1-28) and the burial of the patriarchal figures (24:29-30). An earlier document has been edited by the Deuteronomist to bring the book to a close on a very positive note. Differences from the body of the book, pointing to original independence, can be readily noted, e.g., a military conflict at Jericho (24:11), and the repeated emphasis on the Amorites as the nearly exclusive enemy (24:6, 15).

24:1-28 Covenant renewal

A covenant (in Hebrew *berith*) was the most common form of agreement between nations, groups, or individuals. In the Bible this is extended to God and his people. The earliest biblical precedent for the Joshua covenant was that made with Noah after the flood (Gen 9). This was a unilateral covenant requiring nothing of the contracting party. It was YHWH who pledged himself never to destroy the earth by flood again. The visible sign of this covenant was the rainbow. The covenant with Abraham (Gen 15) can be considered bilateral if the circumcision imposed upon the patriarch is considered part of the agreement (Gen 17:9-14). However the major initiatives come from

delivered them into your power. You took possession of their land, and I destroyed them at your approach. ⁹ Then Balak, son of Zippor, king of Moab, prepared to war against Israel. He summoned Balaam, son of Beor, to curse you, ¹⁰ but I would not listen to Balaam. Instead, he had to bless you, and I delivered you from his power. ¹¹ Once you crossed the Jordan and came to Jericho, the citizens of Jericho fought against you, but I delivered them also into your power. ¹² And I sent the hornets ahead of you which drove them—the Amorites, Perizzites, Canaanites, Hittites, Girgashites, Hivites, and Jebusites—out of your way; it was not your sword or your bow. ¹³ I gave you a land you did not till and cities you did not build, to dwell in; you ate of vineyards and olive groves you did not plant.

¹⁴ "Now, therefore, fear the LORD and serve him completely and sincerely. Cast out the gods your ancestors served beyond the River and in Egypt, and serve the LORD. ¹⁵ If it is displeasing to you to serve the LORD, choose today whom you will serve, the gods your ancestors served beyond the River or the gods of the Amorites in whose country you are dwelling. As for me and my household, we will serve the LORD."

YHWH, who pledges himself to grant Abraham a large and numerous progeny (Gen 14:2-7) and a bountiful country (Gen 15:18-20).

The major covenant is, of course, that of Sinai, which is the prototype of all others (Exod 19–24). Therein, following a customary covenant or treaty form, YHWH presents himself and recounts his benefits (Exod 20:2). He then lists the terms of the agreement (Exod 20:3-17; chs. 21–23). If the terms are agreed upon, YHWH will be the protector and deliverer of his people (Exod 19:5-6). The people agree and in a solemn ritual the covenant is concluded (Exod 24:3-8).

The Joshua covenant renewal takes place in Shechem, one of Israel's central sanctuaries. Following the customary form, there is a recounting of YHWH's saving action, beginning with Abraham and the early settlement of the patriarchs (24:2-4), to Moses and the exodus (24:5-10), and the eventual settlement in Canaan (24:11-13). The recital of this creed placed emphasis on foreign gods and soothsayers, underscoring their ineffectiveness (24:2, 9-11). No mention is made of the pivotal Sinai covenant, as is the case also in other liturgical expressions (e.g., Exod 15). The most likely reason for this is that it would have been redundant and anti-climactic in a ceremony which was itself a covenant ratification. The mention of the hornets leading Israel alludes to Exodus 23:28.

After the litany of the Lord's favorable action, as on Sinai, the people are asked to express their gratitude. Once again the emphasis falls on a strictly monotheistic worship, excluding completely any foreign gods (24:15).

¹⁶But the people answered, "Far be it from us to forsake the LORD to serve other gods. ¹⁷For it was the LORD, our God, who brought us and our ancestors up out of the land of Egypt, out of the house of slavery. He performed those great signs before our very eyes and protected us along our entire journey and among all the peoples through whom we passed. ¹⁸At our approach the LORD drove out all the peoples, including the Amorites who dwelt in the land. Therefore we also will serve the LORD, for he is our God."

¹⁹Joshua in turn said to the people, "You may not be able to serve the LORD, for he is a holy God; he is a passionate God who will not forgive your transgressions or your sins. ²⁰If you forsake the LORD and serve strange gods, he will then do evil to you and destroy you, after having done you good."

²¹But the people answered Joshua, "No! We will serve the LORD." ²²Joshua therefore said to the people, "You are witnesses against yourselves that you have chosen to serve the LORD." They replied, "We are witnesses!" ²³"Now, therefore, put away the foreign gods that are among you and turn your hearts to the LORD, the God of Israel." ²⁴Then the people promised Joshua, "We will serve the LORD, our God, and will listen to his voice."

²⁵So Joshua made a covenant with the people that day and made statutes and ordinances for them at Shechem. ²⁶Joshua wrote these words in the book of the law of God. Then he took a large stone and set it up there under the terebinth that was in the sanctuary of the LORD. ²⁷And Joshua said to all the people, "This stone shall be our witness, for it has heard all the words which the LORD spoke to us. It shall be a witness against you, should you wish to deny your God." ²⁸Then Joshua dismissed the people, each to their own heritage.

Acceptance of the absolute sovereignty of YHWH is initiated by Joshua (24:15) and reaffirmed by the people four times (24:18, 21, 22, 24), a distinct echo of the Sinai agreement (Exod 24:7). The book of the law again comes to the fore (24:25-26; cf. 1:8; 8:30-35), as well as the memorial stone, both related to Sinai (24:26-27; Exod 24:4). With the creedal formula, acceptance by the people, the written terms, and the memorial stone, covenant renewal is complete. The memorial stone is etiological, a perpetual reminder of the covenant bond. It should be noted that a tradition such as this probably reflects also the incorporation of other people encountered in the conquest into the covenant relationship.

Further development of the covenant theme is seen in the later prediction by Jeremiah of a new covenant not written on stone but one which will find a deeply personal response within the human heart (Jer 31:1-34). All of this is brought to a stirring conclusion at the Last Supper when Jesus initiates a new covenant in his blood (Luke 22:20).

Death of Joshua. ²⁹After these events, Joshua, son of Nun, servant of the LORD, died at the age of a hundred and ten, ³⁰and they buried him within the borders of his heritage at Timnath-serah in the mountain region of Ephraim north of Mount Gaash. ³¹Israel served the LORD during the entire lifetime of Joshua, and of those elders who outlived Joshua and who knew all the work the LORD had done for Israel. ³² The bones of Joseph, which the Israelites had brought up from Egypt, were buried in Shechem in the plot of ground Jacob had bought from the sons of Hamor, father of Shechem, for a hundred pieces of money. This was a heritage of the descendants of Joseph. ³³When Eleazar, son of Aaron, also died, he was buried on the hill which had been given to his son Phinehas in the mountain region of Ephraim.

24:29-33

Joshua's death at an advanced age brought the patriarchal period to a close. Patriarchs and priest were laid to rest: Joshua in the land allotted to him in Ephraim (24:30; 19:50), Joseph, whose remains had been brought from Egypt (Gen 50:25), was appropriately buried in Josephite territory (24:32), and Eleazar, son of Aaron, in the mountains of Ephraim (24:33). The chapter as a whole, as well as the burial of Joseph, underscore the importance of Shechem in Israelite history.

The Book of Judges

Were it not for the book of Judges, we would be ignorant of Israelite life from the time of the settlement under Joshua (ca. 1200 B.C.) to the rise of the monarchy (ca. 1050 B.C.). During this span of 150 years considerable importance is attached to the religious and political development of the tribal life of the Israelites. Although not intended as a strict historical presentation, Judges fills in many gaps in its extensive and colorful presentation of the six "major judges" and its summary account of the six "minor judges." This is well before the time of national unity, during a time when the people were bound together solely by their faith in YHWH. This was the period in which the twelve tribes, now settled in various parts of the country, were in the ascendancy and played a singular role in the history of God's people.

The book is divided into three parts: a presentation of tribal coexistence with pagan peoples (1:1–3:6), the accounts of the judges (3:7–16:31), and an appendix with events related to the tribes of Benjamin and Dan (17:1–21:25).

The judges

The Hebrew name of the book, *shopetim*, the participial or substantive form of the verb *shapat*, means to execute justice or to do justice. The notion of judicial magistrates comes to mind at once, but the fact is that none of the judges, with the possible exception of Deborah (4:4), were involved in legal proceedings. Several of them, such as Ibzan, Elon, and Abdon, are said to have "judged Israel," but we are given no explanation of what that means. The major judges are not called such in the text itself, and all of them were involved in acts of liberation. That one of these, Jephthah, is also said to "[have] judged Israel" (12:7) may point to a meaning of "hero" or "savior." The overall relation to justice seems to lie in the fact that they were instruments of God's justice in liberating the people from their enemies, and therefore they may best be seen as liberators or saviors.

Formation and theme

Various documents have been assembled in Judges in something of a patchwork fashion. These existed independently and were brought together from various sources. They include records of Israelite-Canaanite coexistence (ch. 1) and the tales of the charismatic judges from various tribal sources (chs. 3–16). While the judges are regularly spoken of as leading all of Israel, this inflation of personal stature is more editorial than historical. These personalities were all originally identified with particular tribes. There is, furthermore, a list of judges about whom very little is said (e.g., 12:8-13).

The editing of the various strands was the work of the Deuteronomistic school, which has assembled the documents, linked them, and edited the material to point up the major themes of its theological approach. The major idea is the same as that in Joshua, taken from Deuteronomy: infidelity assures defeat, while fidelity is crowned with success. The major motif that sounds throughout Judges has four major moments: sin, punishment, repentance, and deliverance. The Deuteronomist has woven this intricately into his text.

Historical character

Much of Judges reflects early pre-monarchical times, and credence can be accorded to much that it presents regarding the religious, social, and geographical scene. In fact, it surpasses Joshua in more accurately portraying the mix of the Israelite and non-Israelite population long after the occupation. Tribal life dominated Israel's history during this period, as is clearly portrayed in this book.

By the same token, it must be admitted there is a considerable embellishment of the facts in creating the book's *Heldensleben* (i.e., a focus on the life of national heroes) theme. This is clearly seen in the deeds of Judge's principal protagonists. Moreover, major editing has been done to highlight the ideals and values of a later time. In short, the history which is present is always at the service of Deuteronomistic theology.

Theology of Judges

To look to many of the personalities of Judges for ethical inspiration is to look in vain. Ehud is a ruthless murderer who fortunately is on the right side. Jephthah runs a great risk in making his vow and pays the unfortunate price. In a class all by himself, Samson champions the cause of God only in the final moments of his life when he brings catastrophe upon the Philistines. In the main, these are not people on a par with Abraham, Joseph, or Samuel; yet with all their inadequacies, they still play their part in salvation history. They lived before there was national unity, at a time when both the social and religious practices of the Israelites were disorganized and disparate. Their faith was still young; their centers of cult, few; their laws and rituals were still in a formative stage.

The judges play a formidable role. Their stories are an important part of the Bible, and not solely because they link two significant moments in history. In a rudimentary and even crass way, the stories of the judges show the God of Israel still guiding the life of his people. The judges are fully aware of the sacredness of their spiritual allegiance, part of a history which was quite singular. While moral failure met them along the way, they never stood in opposition to YHWH. Repeatedly the Israelites recognized their own wrongdoing and knew that repentance could make things right. And so it did. In the book of Judges the Deuteronomistic thesis is more than vindicated: a people of faith, even if they wander, cannot fail.

The Book of Judges

I. The Situation in Canaan Following the Israelite Conquest

1 **Canaanites in Palestine.** ¹After the death of Joshua the Israelites consulted the LORD, asking, "Who shall be first among us to attack the Canaanites and to do battle with them?" ²The LORD answered: Judah shall attack: I have delivered the land into his power. ³Judah then said to his brother Simeon, "Come up with me into the territory allotted to me, and let us do battle with the Canaanites. I will likewise go with you into the territory allotted to you." So Simeon went with him.

⁴When Judah attacked, the LORD delivered the Canaanites and Perizzites into their power, and they struck down ten thousand of them in Bezek. ⁵They came upon Adonibezek in Bezek and fought against him. When they struck down the Canaanites and Perizzites, ⁶Adonibezek fled. They pursued him, and when they caught him, they cut off

COEXISTENCE

Judges 1:1–3:6

1:1–2:5 A mixed population

The picture of Israel's conquest of the land differs considerably from that depicted in Joshua. By the time of Joshua's death, and much later, there were many pockets of resistance to Israel's presence in the land from indigenous elements that still held sway. This chapter, part of an earlier document, was appended to this section of the Judges narrative at a later date and is, in the main, a credible listing of parts of the country which remained in foreign hands. It is brought into relationship with the preceding volume by the mention of Joshua's death (1:1) in introducing the Judahite campaign. The

▶ This symbol indicates a cross-reference number in the *Catechism of the Catholic Church*. See page 124 for number citations.

his thumbs and big toes. ⁷"Seventy kings," said Adonibezek, "used to pick up scraps under my table with their thumbs and big toes cut off. As I have done, so has God repaid me." He was brought to Jerusalem, and he died there. ⁸The Judahites fought against Jerusalem, captured it, and put it to the sword, setting the city itself on fire.

⁹Afterward the Judahites went down to fight against the Canaanites who lived in the mountain region, in the Negeb, and in the foothills. ¹⁰Judah also marched against the Canaanites who lived in Hebron, which was formerly called Kiriath-arba, and defeated Sheshai, Ahiman, and Talmai. ¹¹They marched from there against the inhabitants of Debir, which was formerly called Kiriath-sepher. ¹²Caleb said, "To the man who attacks Kiriath-sepher and captures it, I will give my daughter Achsah in marriage." ¹³Othniel captured it, the son of Caleb's younger brother Kenaz; so Caleb gave him his daughter Achsah in marriage.

¹⁴When she came to him, she induced him to ask her father for some land. Then, as she alighted from the donkey, Caleb asked her, "What do you want?" ¹⁵She answered, "Give me a present. Since you have put me in the land of the Negeb, give me pools of water." So Caleb gave her what she wanted, both the upper and the lower pool.

¹⁶The descendants of Hobab the Kenite, Moses' father-in-law, came up with the Judahites from the City of Palms to the wilderness of Arad, which is in the Negeb, and they settled among the Amalekites. ¹⁷ Then Judah went with his brother Simeon, and they defeated the Canaanites who lived in Zephath. They put the city under the ban and renamed it Hormah. ¹⁸Judah captured Gaza with its territory, Ashkelon with its territory, Ekron with its territory, and Ashdod with its territory. ¹⁹The LORD was with Judah, so they gained possession of the mountain region. But they could not dispossess those who lived on the plain,

---

desecration of the "mixed population" with its attendant problems moves from south (Judah/Simeon) to north (Dan). The subordination of Simeon to Judah points to its eventual assimilation. The Perizzites (1:4) were not ethnically distinguished from the Canaanites, the name being more descriptive ("unwalled cities") than ethnic. The dismemberment of Adonibezek rendered him incapable of bearing arms at any future date. He shared the fate of many to whom he had meted out the same punishment (1:6-7). The mention of Jerusalem is an erroneous gloss (1:8), contradicting verse 21. David captured Jerusalem at a much later date.

The preeminence of Judah continues in the account of its forays in the south (1:9-13). The wedding gift from Caleb to his daughter in the form of two pools explains the claim of Othniel's descendants in Debir (1:13-15) and parallels the same account in Joshua 15:13-19. Etiology is also dominant in the reference to the Kenites, Moses' in-laws (Num 10:29-32). The efforts of Judah farther north meet with only limited success. They took the hill

because they had iron chariots. ²⁰As Moses had commanded, they gave Hebron to Caleb, who then drove the three sons of Anak away from there.

²¹As for the Jebusites dwelling in Jerusalem, the Benjaminites did not dispossess them, so that the Jebusites live with the Benjaminites in Jerusalem to the present day.

²²The house of Joseph, too, went up against Bethel, and the LORD was with them. ²³The house of Joseph reconnoitered Bethel, which formerly was called Luz. ²⁴The scouts saw a man coming out of the city and said to him, "Tell us the way into the city, and we will show you mercy." ²⁵He showed them the way into the city, and they put the city to the sword; but they let the man and his whole clan go free. ²⁶The man then went to the land of the Hittites, where he built a city and called it Luz, which is its name to this day.

²⁷Manasseh did not take possession of Beth-shean with its towns or of Taanach with its towns. Nor did they dispossess the inhabitants of Dor and its towns, those of Ibleam and its towns, or those of Megiddo and its towns. The Canaan-ites continued to live in this district. ²⁸When Israel grew stronger, they conscripted the Canaanites as laborers, but did not actually drive them out. ²⁹Ephraim did not drive out the Canaanites living in Gezer, and so the Canaanites lived among them in Gezer.

³⁰Nor did Zebulun dispossess the inhabitants of Kitron or those of Nahalol; the Canaanites lived among them and became forced laborers.

³¹Nor did Asher dispossess the inhabitants of Acco or those of Sidon, or take possession of Mahaleb, Achzib, Helbah, Aphik, or Rehob. ³²So the Asherites settled among the Canaanite inhabitants of the land, for they had not dispossessed them.

³³Nor did Naphtali drive out the inhabitants of Beth-shemesh or those of Beth-anath. They settled among the Canaanite inhabitants of the land and the inhabitants of Beth-shemesh and Beth-anath became forced laborers for them.

³⁴The Amorites hemmed in the Danites in the mountain region, not permitting them to come down onto the plain. ³⁵So the Amorites continued to live

---

country (1:17-20) but had no success on the coastal plain and gained no access to Philistine territory.

Indigenous populations were not dislodged in the territories of Benjamin (1:21), Ephraim and Manasseh (1:22-29), Zebulun (1:30), Asher (1:31-32), Naphtali (1:33), and Dan (1:34-36). Mention is made, however, that some of the native population were pressed into slave labor by the Israelites (1:35).

The reason for this ambivalent picture of the occupation is explained at the beginning of chapter 2 (vv. 1-5), and it is clearly Deuteronomistic. In view of their disobedience to the Lord's wishes and their entrance into forbidden pacts with the resident population, the Israelites were unsuccessful in making the land their own. This message was relayed by a divine messenger at Bochim, an unidentified locale but perhaps related to the

in Harheres, Aijalon, and Shaalbim, but as the power of the house of Joseph grew, they were conscripted as laborers.

³⁶The territory of the Amorites extended from the Akrabbim pass, from Sela and upward.

2 **Infidelities of the Israelites.** ¹A messenger of the LORD went up from Gilgal to Bochim and said, I brought you up from Egypt and led you into the land which I promised on oath to your ancestors. I said, I will never break my covenant with you, ²but you must not make a covenant with the inhabitants of this land; you must pull down their altars. But you did not listen to me. Look what you have done! ³For I also said, I will not clear them out of your way; they will become traps for you, and their gods a snare for you.

⁴When the messenger of the LORD had spoken these things to all the Israelites, the people wept aloud. ⁵They named that place Bochim, and they offered sacrifice there to the LORD.

⁶Then Joshua dismissed the people, and the Israelites went, each to their own heritage, to take possession of the land. ⁷The people served the LORD during the entire lifetime of Joshua, and of those elders who outlived Joshua and who had seen all the great work the LORD had done for Israel. ⁸Joshua, son of Nun, the servant of the LORD, died at the age of a hundred and ten, ⁹and they buried him within the borders of his heritage at Timnath-heres in the mountain region of Ephraim north of Mount Gaash.

¹⁰When the rest of that generation were also gathered to their ancestors,

---

important sanctuary at Bethel. The name, however, is significant; it is related to the Hebrew verb "to weep." Bochim then is "weeper's land," a lasting reminder of Israel's infidelity.

2:6-36 The apostasy of Israel

The chapter is the Deuteronomist's introduction to the book as a whole. It picks up where Joshua ended, with the death and burial of Joshua (2:8-9 cf. Josh 24:29-32) and the retirement of the tribes to their designated territories (2:6; Josh 13–19). This supports the thesis that the first chapter of Judges was a late addition, perhaps placed here for historical reasons.

The continued presence of pagan elements is explained solely in terms of Israel's wanton disregard of YHWH's commands. The population is cited as the generation that followed Joshua, a generation which departed from the fidelity of their predecessors (2:7, 10). Not adhering to the faith of their forebears, this generation turned to idolatry in the worship of Canaanite gods, as well as the gods of neighboring countries (2:10-13). Baal (a word which means "lord") was the chief god of the Canaanite pantheon and Astarte, his consort, was the goddess of love and fertility. The plural references here look to the various forms and images of the two which were used in popular worship, rather than a plurality of deities (2:11, 13).

and a later generation arose that did not know the Lord or the work he had done for Israel, ¹¹the Israelites did what was evil in the sight of the Lord. They served the Baals, ¹²and abandoned the Lord, the God of their ancestors, the one who had brought them out of the land of Egypt. They followed other gods, the gods of the peoples around them, and bowed down to them, and provoked the Lord.

¹³Because they had abandoned the Lord and served Baal and the Astartes, ¹⁴the anger of the Lord flared up against Israel, and he delivered them into the power of plunderers who despoiled them. He sold them into the power of the enemies around them, and they were no longer able to withstand their enemies. ¹⁵Whenever they marched out, the hand of the Lord turned against them, as the Lord had said, and as the Lord had sworn to them; and they were in great distress. ¹⁶But the Lord raised up judges to save them from the power of their plunderers; ¹⁷but they did not listen to their judges either, for they prostituted themselves by following other gods, bowing down to them. They were quick to stray from the way their ancestors had taken, who obeyed the commandments of the Lord; but these did not. ¹⁸When the Lord raised up judges for them, he would be with the judge and save them from the power of their enemies as long as the judge lived. The Lord would change his mind when they groaned in their affliction under their oppressors. ¹⁹But when the judge died, they would again do worse than their ancestors, following other gods, serving and bowing down to them, relinquishing none of their evil practices or stubborn ways.

²⁰The anger of the Lord flared up against Israel, and he said: Because this nation has transgressed my covenant, which I enjoined on their ancestors, and has not listened to me, ²¹I for my part will not clear away for them any more of the nations Joshua left when he died.

The judges were raised up to deliver the oppressed people. In a departure from the common motif of sin-punishment-conversion-deliverance, there is no explicit mention here of conversion ("crying to the Lord"); repentance is at best implicit. The deliverance is simply an act of yhwh's pity (2:18). Variations in the narrative also point to different sources. In one instance, the people failed to pay any heed to the judges but simply abandoned themselves to their pagan practices (2:17); in another, there is recidivism or backsliding after deliverance when the judge dies (2:18-19). In any case, the foreign nations remained in place as a continued test of the people's fidelity (2:20-23). Testing was necessary since the present generation had not participated in the battles under Joshua (3:2).

Israel's hostile neighbors included the Philistines on the central coastal plain, Canaanites throughout the country, and the citizens of Lebanon in the north (3:2-3). The stereotypical list of non-Israelites affords little knowledge of the actual identity of some of them (3:5; cf. Josh 3:10; 24:11). At the time there was both cultic abuse and inter-marriage as well (3:6). In all of

²²They will be made to test Israel, to see whether or not they will keep to the way of the LORD and continue in it as their ancestors did. ²³Therefore the LORD allowed these nations to remain instead of expelling them immediately. He had not delivered them into the power of Joshua.

3 ¹These are the nations the LORD allowed to remain, so that through them he might test Israel, all those who had not experienced any of the Canaanite wars— ²to teach warfare to those generations of Israelites who had never experienced it: ³the five lords of the Philistines, and all the Canaanites, the Sidonians, and the Hivites who lived in the mountain region of the Lebanon between Baal-hermon and Lebo-hamath. ⁴These served as a test for Israel, to know whether they would obey the commandments the LORD had enjoined on their ancestors through Moses. ⁵So the Israelites settled among the Canaanites, Hittites, Amorites, Perizzites, Hivites, and Jebusites. ⁶They took their daughters in marriage, and gave their own daughters to their sons in marriage, and served their gods.

II. Stories of the Judges

Othniel. ⁷Then the Israelites did what was evil in the sight of the LORD; they forgot the LORD, their God, and served the Baals and the Asherahs, ⁸and the anger of the LORD flared up against them. He sold them into the power of Cushan-rishathaim, king of Aram Naharaim; and the Israelites served Cushan-rishathaim for eight years. ⁹But when the Israelites cried out to the LORD, he raised up a savior for them, to save them. It was Othniel, son of Caleb's younger brother Kenaz. ¹⁰The spirit of the LORD came upon him, and he judged Israel. When he marched out to war, the LORD delivered Cushan-rishathaim,

---

this, the Deuteronomist's point is clear. The people in exile for whom he writes, one half of a millennium later, should see their unfortunate lot as a part of a continuous history of infidelity. The continued presence of pagan elements was due not to YHWH's original design but to human sinfulness.

THE JUDGES

Judges 3:7–16:31

3:7-11 Othniel

Little is said about the first of the judges. Othniel is a paradigm of much that is to follow: the people sin, YHWH punishes, the people turn to the Lord, YHWH sends a deliverer. This introductory piece is probably Judahite in origin, with Othniel's origin found in the Calebite clan of Judah. Neither the king nor the location of his kingdom can be identified with certainty. Central to the account is the spirit of the Lord which takes possession of the judge (3:10), a divine force which enters into the Lord's emissary enabling him or her to perform feats beyond any human expectations.

king of Aram, into his power, and his hold on Cushan-rishathaim was firm. ¹¹So the land was at rest for forty years, until Othniel, son of Kenaz, died.

Ehud. ¹²Again the Israelites did what was evil in the sight of the LORD, so he strengthened Eglon, king of Moab, against Israel because they did what was evil in the sight of the LORD. ¹³Taking the Ammonites and Amalek as allies, he went and defeated Israel, taking possession of the City of Palms. ¹⁴So the Israelites served Eglon, king of Moab, for eighteen years.

¹⁵But when the Israelites cried out to the LORD, he raised up for them a savior, Ehud, son of Gera, a Benjaminite who was left-handed. The Israelites would send their tribute to Eglon, king of Moab, by him. ¹⁶Ehud made himself a two-edged dagger a foot long, and strapped it under his clothes on his right thigh. ¹⁷He presented the tribute to Eglon, king of Moab; now Eglon was a very fat man. ¹⁸When he had finished presenting the tribute, he dismissed the troops who had carried the tribute. ¹⁹But he himself turned back at the sculptured stones near Gilgal, and said, "I have a secret message for you, O king." And the king said, "Silence!" Then when all his attendants had left his presence, ²⁰Ehud went in to him where he sat alone in his cool upper room. Ehud said, "I have a word from God for you." So the king rose from his throne. ²¹Then Ehud with his left hand drew the dagger from his right thigh, and thrust it into Eglon's belly. ²²The hilt also went in after the blade, and the fat closed over the blade because he did not withdraw the dagger from the body.

²³Then Ehud went out onto the porch, shutting the doors of the upper room on Eglon and locking them. ²⁴When Ehud had left and the servants had come, they saw that the doors of the upper room were locked, and thought, "He must be easing himself in the cool chamber."

3:12-30 Ehud

The story of Ehud's triumph over Eglon, king of Moab, seemingly existed originally as an account of bravado on the part of a rustic Israelite in effectively countering the king of a hostile Transjordanian realm. This is contained in the murder narrative (3:15-25), quite complete in itself, which was then adapted to fit the basic Judges framework.

The threat from an expanding Israel aroused its Transjordanian neighbors and led to its subjugation for eighteen years, but the defeat is attributed to Israel's moral waywardness (3:12-14). Then Ehud of Benjamin is designated by the Lord, without any mention, however, of his receiving the spirit. His left-handedness would have been considered a human defect or imperfection, which in this case proved an asset in enabling him to conceal his dagger on his right thigh (3:16) The account is somewhat gross in its bloody description of the fat king's death (3:22); and its humor coarse in the servants' imagining that the king was relieving himself (3:24). However, it would have been seen as a striking example of YHWH's power over an evil

²⁵They waited until they were at a loss when he did not open the doors of the upper room. So they took the key and opened them, and there was their lord lying on the floor, dead.

²⁶During their delay Ehud escaped and, passing the sculptured stones, took refuge in Seirah. ²⁷On his arrival he sounded the horn in the mountain region of Ephraim, and the Israelites went down from the mountains with him as their leader. ²⁸"Follow me," he said to them, "for the LORD has delivered your enemies the Moabites into your power." So they followed him down and seized the fords of the Jordan against the Moabites, permitting no one to cross. ²⁹On that oc-casion they slew about ten thousand Moabites, all of them strong warriors. Not one escaped. ³⁰So Moab was brought under the power of Israel at that time; and the land had rest for eighty years.

Shamgar. ³¹After him there was Shamgar, son of Anath, who slew six hundred Philistines with an oxgoad. He, too, was a savior for Israel.

Deborah and Barak. ¹The Israelites again did what was evil in the sight of the LORD; Ehud was dead. ²So the LORD sold them into the power of the Canaanite king, Jabin, who reigned in Hazor. The general of his army was Sisera, who lived in Harosheth-ha-goiim. ³But the Israelites cried out to the LORD;

---

opponent, even to the point of ridicule. There is drama in the narrative, seen in the ruse Ehud uses to see the king alone, the impending death described as a message, the departure of Ehud with doors locked behind him, and the king inaccessible until he is certainly dead.

The account ends on a note of military prowess. Ehud drew on Ephraimite forces and subdued the forces of Moab, resulting in an eighty-year period of peace (3:26-30).

A single verse is given to the judge Shamgar, who followed Ehud and was engaged in military exploits against the Philistines (3:31).

Chapters 4–5 Deborah

The account of Israel's woman judge comes to us in two forms, one prose (ch. 4) and the other, a poetic canticle (ch. 5). The latter, although at times unclear due to errors in literary transmission, is one of the oldest extant pieces of poetry, thought to be written very close to the time of the events depicted. The two accounts converge around essentials but are at variance in secondary features. In the narrative, the principal characters on the positive side are Deborah, Barak, and Jael. As judges, the roles of Deborah and Barak coalesce. Although the victory is his, the direction is hers. Although the action of Jael is applauded, she is not considered a judge. Her story seems to have arisen out of a context of tales of popular heroism. The two antagonists are Jabin and Sisera.

for with his nine hundred iron chariots Jabin harshly oppressed the Israelites for twenty years.

⁴At that time the prophet Deborah, wife of Lappidoth, was judging Israel. ⁵She used to sit under Deborah's palm tree, between Ramah and Bethel in the mountain region of Ephraim, where the Israelites came up to her for judgment. ⁶She had Barak, son of Abinoam, summoned from Kedesh of Naphtali. She said to him, "This is what the LORD, the God of Israel, commands: Go, march against Mount Tabor, and take with you ten thousand men from Naphtali and Zebulun. ⁷I will draw Sisera, the general of Jabin's army, out to you at the Wadi Kishon, together with his chariots and troops, and I will deliver them into your power." ⁸But Barak answered her, "If you come with me, I will go; if you do not come with me, I will not go." ⁹"I will certainly go with you," she replied, "but you will not gain glory for the expedition on which you are setting out, for it is into a woman's power that the LORD is going to sell Sisera." So Deborah arose and went with Barak and journeyed with him to Kedesh.

¹⁰Barak summoned Zebulun and Naphtali to Kedesh, and ten thousand men followed him. Deborah also went up with him. ¹¹Now Heber the Kenite had detached himself from Cain, the descendants of Hobab, Moses' father-in-law, and had pitched his tent by the terebinth of Zaanannim, which was near Kedesh.

¹²It was reported to Sisera that Barak, son of Abinoam, had gone up to Mount Tabor. ¹³So Sisera called out all nine hundred of his iron chariots and all his forces from Harosheth-ha-goiim to the Wadi Kishon. ¹⁴Deborah then said to Barak, "Up! This is the day on which the LORD has delivered Sisera into your power. The LORD marches before you." So Barak went down Mount Tabor, followed by his ten thousand men. ¹⁵And the LORD threw Sisera and all his chariots and forces into a panic before Barak. Sisera himself dismounted from his chariot and fled on foot, ¹⁶but Barak pursued the chariots and the army as far as Harosheth-ha-goiim. The entire army of Sisera fell beneath the sword, not even one man surviving.

¹⁷Sisera fled on foot to the tent of Jael, wife of Heber the Kenite, for there was peace between Jabin, king of Hazor, and

4:1-23 The prose account

Contained within a Deuteronomistic introduction (4:1-3) and conclusion (4:23), the chapter is made up of battle preparations (4:1-9), the battle itself (4:10-16), and the death of Sisera (4:17-21). The provenance is in the north from Bethel in Ephraim (4:4) to Hazor, north of the sea of Galilee (4:2). To speak of Jabin as the "Canaanite king" (4:2) is as much an overstatement as it is to call the tribal battles of the book the responses of "Israel." He is more accurately seen as the Canaanite king of Hazor. A Jabin of Hazor has been met before and overcome by Joshua (Josh 11); his name may have anachronistically attached itself to the present tradition. Attention passes quickly to Jabin's military leader, Sisera, whose non-Canaanite name may well be of Philistine origin (4:2).

the family of Heber the Kenite. [18]Jael went out to meet Sisera and said to him, "Turn aside, my lord, turn aside with me; do not be afraid." So he went into her tent, and she covered him with a rug. [19]He said to her, "Please give me a little water to drink. I am thirsty." So she opened a skin of milk, gave him a drink, and then covered him. [20]"Stand at the entrance of the tent," he said to her. "If anyone comes and asks, 'Is there someone here?' say, 'No!'" [21]Jael, wife of Heber, got a tent peg and took a mallet in her hand. When Sisera was in a deep sleep from exhaustion, she approached him stealthily and drove the peg through his temple and down into the ground, and he died. [22]Then when Barak came in pursuit of Sisera, Jael went out to meet him and said to him, "Come, I will show you the man you are looking for." So he went in with her, and there lay Sisera dead, with the tent peg through his temple.

[23]Thus on that day God humbled the Canaanite king, Jabin, before the Israelites; [24]their power weighed ever more heavily on him, until at length they finished off the Canaanite king, Jabin.

Deborah was a prophetess and a judge, exercising a threefold office in the account. As a prophetess, she was a diviner of the divine will (4:4); she also handed down judicial sentences (4:5); and she was a charismatic leader (judge) as well. Barak is summoned by Deborah to assume a "judging" role by YHWH's design, i.e., the liberation of his people from Canaanite oppression (4:6-7; cf. Heb. 11:32). Barak's plea for Deborah's presence is an effort to place Sisera's defeat clearly in YHWH's camp, with his falling into "a woman's power" (4:8-9). In the battle itself Deborah plays only a directive role; the actual victory is Barak's. The battle takes place at the Kishon river on the Plain of Esdraelon in the region of Mt. Tabor, placing the event clearly in relationship to the north (4:12-13).

The parenthetical mention of the Kenites, Moses' in-laws (Num 10:29), serves to introduce Jael at a later point (4:17). The Kenites originally settled in southern Judah (1:16), with a segment separating and settling in the north (4:11).

With the defeat of Jabin's forces, attention passes to the fate of his general Sisera. Like the story of Ehud in the previous chapter, this has all the characteristics of an epic tale which originally constituted a separate and isolated account. It is here attached to Deborah and Barak possibly for historical reasons, but more importantly for theological emphasis. It is a woman ally of the Hebrews who, even though she violates the important law of hospitality, overcomes pagan military prowess with a tent peg (4:17-22)! Barak's pursuit proves unnecessary. Not a warrior's might but the hand of a woman had dispatched the enemy. It was another victory for YHWH. Later, in the face of disgrace and defeat, Jabin himself succumbed (4:23).

"[Deborah] said, . . . 'Go, march against Mount Tabor, and take with you ten thousand men . . .'" (Judg 4:6). Mount Tabor is also the scene of Jesus' transfiguration (Luke 9:28ff).

5 Song of Deborah.

Song of Deborah. ¹On that day Deborah sang this song—and Barak, son of Abinoam:

²When uprising broke out in Israel,
when the people rallied for
duty—bless the Lord!
³Hear, O kings! Give ear, O princes!
I will sing, I will sing to the
Lord,
I will make music to the Lord,
the God of Israel.
⁴Lord, when you went out from Seir,
when you marched from the
plains of Edom,
The earth shook, the heavens poured,
the clouds poured rain,
⁵The mountains streamed,
before the Lord, the One of
Sinai,
before the Lord, the God of
Israel.
⁶In the days of Shamgar, son of
Anath,
in the days of Jael, caravans
ceased:
Those who traveled the roads
now traveled by roundabout
paths.
⁷Gone was freedom beyond the
walls,

gone indeed from Israel.
When I, Deborah, arose,
when I arose, a mother in Israel.
⁸New gods were their choice;
then war was at the gates.
No shield was to be found, no spear,
among forty thousand in Israel!
⁹My heart is with the leaders of
Israel,
with the dedicated ones of the
people—bless the Lord;
¹⁰Those who ride on white donkeys,
seated on saddle rugs,
and those who travel the road,
Sing of them
¹¹to the sounds of musicians at
the wells.
There they recount the just deeds of
the Lord,
his just deeds bringing freedom
to Israel.
¹²Awake, awake, Deborah!
Awake, awake, strike up a song!
Arise, Barak!
Take captive your captors, son
of Abinoam!
¹³Then down went Israel against the
mighty,
the army of the Lord went
down for him against the
warriors.

5:1-31 The poetic account: Deborah's canticle

This is basically an ancient victory song (5:12-30), given a cultic setting as a hymn of thanks (5:1-11, 31). An ancient piece of Hebrew poetry, it focuses on the victory attained in chapter 4.

This is the song of Deborah and Barak, the charismatic leaders of the preceding chapter (5:1). Formerly Barak had been engaged in the battle; here he is largely an onlooker in a battle which is fought by yhwh, the warrior God. The Lord makes his entry from the south, from Sinai through Edom, accompanied by the cataclysms of nature which are regularly the trappings of mythological poetry (5:4-5). He comes to liberate a people reduced to slavery, excluded from human commerce and contact (5:6-7); yet, in true

¹⁴From Ephraim, their base in the
valley;
behind you, Benjamin, among
your troops.
From Machir came down commanders,
from Zebulun wielders of the
marshal's staff.
¹⁵The princes of Issachar were with
Deborah,
Issachar, faithful to Barak;
in the valley they followed at his
heels.
Among the clans of Reuben
great were the searchings of
heart!
¹⁶Why did you stay beside your
hearths
listening to the lowing of the
herds?
Among the clans of Reuben
great were the searchings of
heart!
¹⁷Gilead stayed beyond the Jordan;
Why did Dan spend his time in
ships?
Asher remained along the shore,
he stayed in his havens.

¹⁸Zebulun was a people who defied
death,
Naphtali, too, on the open
heights!
¹⁹The kings came and fought;
then they fought, those kings of
Canaan,
At Taanach by the waters of
Megiddo;
no spoil of silver did they take.
²⁰From the heavens the stars fought;
from their courses they fought
against Sisera.
²¹The Wadi Kishon swept them away;
the wadi overwhelmed them,
the Wadi Kishon.
Trample down the strong!
²²Then the hoofs of the horses
hammered,
the galloping, galloping of
steeds.
²³"Curse Meroz," says the messenger
of the LORD,
"curse, curse its inhabitants!
For they did not come when the
LORD helped,
the help of the LORD against the
warriors."

Deuteronomistic fashion, the cause of disaster is Israel's own apostasy. It has left the people bereft of any form of self-defense (5:8). It is the ingenuity of Deborah which now galvanizes Israel's forces (5:9-11).

The location of the battle is Taanach on the Kishon, the same region identified in chapter 4 (5:19-21). In the prose account, however, the forces were drawn from Zebulun and Naphtali; here it is extended to Ephraim, Benjamin, Manasseh (Machir), and Issachar (5:14-15a). Reproved are the tribes that failed to respond: the Transjordanians, as well as Dan, Asher, and the unidentified locale of Meroz (5:15b-17, 23). It is clear that the battle has taken on national proportions in the hymn, yet no mention is made of Judah, which may have already begun its independent stance.

It is the forces of nature that combine to spell defeat for the Canaanites, with the role of the military left undefined (5:19-20). This is clearly YHWH's victory.

²⁴Most blessed of women is Jael,
the wife of Heber the Kenite,
blessed among tent-dwelling
women!
²⁵He asked for water, she gave him
milk,
in a princely bowl she brought
him curds.
²⁶With her hand she reached for the
peg,
with her right hand, the work-
man's hammer.
She hammered Sisera, crushed his
head;
she smashed, pierced his temple.
²⁷At her feet he sank down, fell, lay
still;
down at her feet he sank and fell;
where he sank down, there he
fell, slain.

²⁸From the window she looked down,
the mother of Sisera peered
through the lattice:
"Why is his chariot so long in coming?
why are the hoofbeats of his
chariots delayed?"
²⁹The wisest of her princesses an-
swers her;

she even replies to herself,
³⁰"They must be dividing the spoil
they took:
a slave woman or two for each
man,
Spoil of dyed cloth for Sisera,
spoil of ornate dyed cloth,
a pair of ornate dyed cloths for
my neck in the spoil."

³¹So perish all your enemies, O
LORD!
But may those who love you be
like the sun rising in its
might!

And the land was at rest for forty years.

6 The Call of Gideon. ¹The Israelites did what was evil in the sight of the LORD, who therefore delivered them into the power of Midian for seven years, ²so that Midian held Israel subject. From fear of Midian the Israelites made dens in the mountains, the caves, and the strongholds. ³For it used to be that whenever the Israelites had completed sowing their crops, Midian, Amalek, and the Kedemites would come up, ⁴encamp against them, and lay waste the produce

---

The account of Jael is Hebrew poetry at its most vivid, with its striking contrast between the generous offering of refreshment and the cunning of the plan to kill (5:25-26). More than touching is the description of Sisera's mother awaiting his return from battle, with its feminine conjectures on the reason for the delay—that the victors are dividing the spoils—an imagining far from reality.

The dichotomous final plea prays for misfortune to plague the evil-doer and blessings to surround the observant, an oft-repeated Hebrew invocation.

Chapters 6–9 Gideon and Abimelech

The complexity of the Gideon narrative is rooted in various distinct and even disparate sources which are here interwoven. It appears evident that

of the land as far as the outskirts of Gaza, leaving no sustenance in Israel, and no sheep, ox, or donkey. ⁵For they would come up with their livestock, and their tents would appear as thick as locusts. They would be too many to count when they came into the land to lay it waste. ⁶Israel was reduced to utter poverty by Midian, and so the Israelites cried out to the LORD.

⁷When Israel cried out to the LORD because of Midian, ⁸the LORD sent a prophet to the Israelites who said to them: Thus says the LORD, the God of Israel: I am the one who brought you up from Egypt; I brought you out of the house of slavery. ⁹I rescued you from the power of Egypt and all your oppressors. I drove them out before you and gave you their land. ¹⁰And I said to you: I, the LORD, am your God; you shall not fear the gods of the Amorites in whose land you are dwelling. But you did not listen to me.

¹¹Then the messenger of the LORD came and sat under the terebinth in Ophrah that belonged to Joash the Abiezrite. Joash's son Gideon was beating out wheat in the wine press to save it from the Midianites, ¹²and the messenger of the LORD appeared to him and said: The LORD is with you, you mighty warrior! ¹³"My lord," Gideon said to him, "if the LORD is with us, why has all this happened to us? Where are his wondrous deeds about which our ancestors told us when they said, 'Did not the LORD bring us up from Egypt?' For now the LORD has abandoned us and has delivered us into the power of Midian." ¹⁴The LORD turned to him and said: Go with the strength you have, and save Israel from the power of Midian. Is it not I who send you? ¹⁵But he answered him, "Please, my Lord, how can I save Israel? My family is the poorest in Manasseh, and I am the most insignificant in my father's house." ¹⁶The LORD said to him: I will be with you, and you will cut down Midian to the last man. ¹⁷He answered him, "If you look on me with favor, give me a sign that you are the one speaking with me. ¹⁸Please do not depart from here until I come to you and bring out my offering and set it before you." He answered: I will await your return.

¹⁹So Gideon went off and prepared a young goat and an ephah of flour in the form of unleavened cakes. Putting the meat in a basket and the broth in a pot,

the Gideon (chs. 6–8) and Abimelech (ch. 9) stories were originally separate and unrelated narratives, with many authors seeing the link based on family ties as being artificial (8:31). Gideon clearly fits the profile of a judge; Abimelech is simply an example of a failed attempt at kingship. Other sources will be indicated at a later point; they blur but do not extinguish the basic idea: the blessings of virtue and the tragedy of evil.

6:1-40 Gideon's call and mission

The threat at this point comes from the Midianties, a people related to Moses by marriage (Exod 18:1), who proved to be more than a thorn in his side during the exodus experience (Num 25:6-18; ch. 31). They were a

he brought them out to him under the terebinth and presented them. ²⁰The messenger of God said to him: Take the meat and unleavened cakes and lay them on this rock; then pour out the broth. When he had done so, ²¹the messenger of the LORD stretched out the tip of the staff he held. When he touched the meat and unleavened cakes, a fire came up from the rock and consumed the meat and unleavened cakes. Then the messenger of the LORD disappeared from sight. ²²Gideon, now aware that it had been the messenger of the LORD, said, "Alas, Lord GOD, that I have seen the messenger of the LORD face to face!" ²³The LORD answered him: You are safe. Do not fear. You shall not die. ²⁴So Gideon built there an altar to the LORD and called it Yahweh-shalom. To this day it is still in Ophrah of the Abiezrites.

²⁵That same night the LORD said to him: Take your father's bull, the bull fattened for seven years, and pull down your father's altar to Baal. As for the asherah beside it, cut it down ²⁶and build an altar to the LORD, your God, on top of this stronghold with the pile of wood. Then take the fattened bull and offer it as a whole-burnt sacrifice on the wood from the asherah you have cut down. ²⁷So Gideon took ten of his servants and did as the LORD had commanded him. But he was too afraid of his family and of the townspeople to do it by day; he did it at night. ²⁸Early the next morning the townspeople found that the altar of Baal had been dismantled, the asherah beside it cut down, and the fattened bull offered on the altar that was built. ²⁹They asked one another, "Who did this?" They inquired and searched until they were told, "Gideon, son of Joash, did it." ³⁰So the townspeople said to Joash, "Bring out your son that he may die, for he has dismantled the altar of Baal and cut down the asherah that was beside it." ³¹But Joash replied to all who were standing around him, "Is it for you to take action for Baal, or be his savior? Anyone who takes action for him shall be put to death by morning. If he is a god, let him act for himself, since his altar has been dismantled!" ³²So on that

---

nomadic people largely identified with the Sinai peninsula who, with other tribes, were making incursions into Israel.

Oppressed by the Midianites, Israel cried out to the Lord, and this leads to the call of Gideon. The Lord's messenger (6:11) is actually YHWH himself (6:14,16). Like Jacob before him (Gen 32:31), Gideon is granted this visible contact without incurring death (6:22-23). Before accepting his call, Gideon asks for a sign, a literary device which allows for the introduction of two distinct sources. The two are etiologies, one explaining the name of the altar at Ophrah (6:19-24; "the Lord is peace"), the other explaining Gideon's name change (6:25-32; Jerubbaal means "Let Baal take action"). The first authenticates the call of Gideon through the fiery consumption of the offering; the second, the successful destruction of the pagan altar and sacred poles, connected with the cult of Astarte, the female fertility goddess (6:25;

82

apostasy
punishment
repentance
restoration

day Gideon was called Jerubbaal, because of the words, "Let Baal take action against him, since he dismantled his altar."

[33]Then all Midian and Amalek and the Kedemites mustered and crossed over into the valley of Jezreel, where they encamped. [34]And Gideon was clothed with the spirit of the LORD, and he blew the horn summoning Abiezer to follow him. [35]He sent messengers throughout Manasseh, and they, too, were summoned to follow him; he also sent messengers throughout Asher, Zebulun, and Naphtali, and they advanced to meet the others. [36]Gideon said to God, "If indeed you are going to save Israel through me, as you have said, [37]I am putting this woolen fleece on the threshing floor, and if dew is on the fleece alone, while all the ground is dry, I shall know that you will save Israel through me, as you have said." [38]That is what happened. Early the next morning when he wrung out the fleece, he squeezed enough dew from it to fill a bowl. [39]Gideon then said to God, "Do not be angry with me if I speak once more. Let me make just one more test with the fleece. Let the fleece alone be dry, but let there be dew on all the ground." [40]That

is what God did that night: the fleece alone was dry, but there was dew on all the ground.

7 Defeat of Midian. [1]Early the next morning Jerubbaal (that is, Gideon) encamped by the spring of Harod with all his soldiers. The camp of Midian was north of him, beside the hill of Moreh in the valley. [2]The LORD said to Gideon: You have too many soldiers with you for me to deliver Midian into their power, lest Israel vaunt itself against me and say, "My own power saved me." [3]So announce in the hearing of the soldiers, "If anyone is afraid or fearful, let him leave! Let him depart from Mount Gilead!" Twenty-two thousand of the soldiers left, but ten thousand remained. [4]The LORD said to Gideon: There are still too many soldiers. Lead them down to the water and I will test them for you there. If I tell you that a certain man is to go with you, he must go with you. But no one is to go if I tell you he must not. [5]When Gideon led the soldiers down to the water, the LORD said to him: Everyone who laps up the water as a dog does with its tongue you shall set aside by himself; and everyone who kneels down to drink raising his hand to his mouth you shall set aside by himself. [6]Those

---

cf. Exod 34:13), and the construction of a new altar. The failure of Baal to act in his own defense explains Gideon's name change (6:32).

The Lord's spirit takes possession of Gideon as he goes forth to battle (6:34). Even with the help of four tribes (6:35), the skeptical judge still seeks assurance of victory, which is granted in the signs of the wet and dry fleece (6:36-40).

7:1-23 War with the Midianites

The Israelites are now battle ready. However, a significant reduction in forces takes place first. If YHWH was to be recognized as the victor, human

who lapped up the water with their tongues numbered three hundred, but all the rest of the soldiers knelt down to drink the water. ⁷The LORD said to Gideon: By means of the three hundred who lapped up the water I will save you and deliver Midian into your power. So let all the other soldiers go home. ⁸They took up such supplies as the soldiers had with them, as well as their horns, and Gideon sent the rest of the Israelites to their tents, but kept the three hundred men. Now the camp of Midian was below him in the valley.

⁹That night the LORD said to Gideon: Go, descend on the camp, for I have delivered it into your power. ¹⁰If you are afraid to attack, go down to the camp with your aide Purah ¹¹and listen to what they are saying. After that you will have the courage to descend on the camp. So he went down with his aide Purah to the outposts of the armed men in the camp. ¹²The Midianites, Amalekites, and all the Kedemites were lying in the valley, thick as locusts. Their camels could not be counted, for they were as many as the sands on the seashore. ¹³When Gideon arrived, one man was telling another about a dream. "I had a dream," he said, "that a round loaf of barley bread was rolling into the camp of Midian. It came to a certain tent and struck it and turned it upside down, and the tent collapsed." ¹⁴"This can only be the sword of the Israelite Gideon, son of Joash," the other replied. "God has delivered Midian and all the camp into his power." ¹⁵When Gideon heard the account of the dream and its explanation, he bowed down. Then returning to the camp of Israel, he said, "Arise, for the LORD has delivered the camp of Midian into your power."

¹⁶He divided the three hundred men into three companies, and provided them all with horns and with empty jars and torches inside the jars. ¹⁷"Watch me and follow my lead," he told them. "I shall go to the edge of the camp, and as I do, you must do also. ¹⁸When I and those with me blow horns, you too must blow horns all around the camp and cry out, 'For the LORD and for Gideon!'" ¹⁹So Gideon and the hundred men who were with him came to the edge of the camp at the beginning of the middle watch, just after the posting of the guards. They blew the horns and broke the jars they were holding. ²⁰When the three companies had blown their horns and broken their jars, they took the torches in their left hands, and in their right the horns

---

forces had to be reduced (7:2). The fearful were sent home, leaving a force of ten thousand (7:3). Further reduction was obtained by distinguishing between those who drank water with cupped hands and heads erect and those who bent down to drink. The more cautious and alert "heads up" group remained, whereas the others were dismissed. This reduced Gideon's forces to three hundred men (7:6-8).

A spying foray into enemy territory led to Gideon's hearing the dream recounted; it clearly pointed to an Israelite victory, with the barley loaf standing for the agricultural Israel (7:9-15). The battle took place with no

they had been blowing, and cried out, "A sword for the LORD and for Gideon!" [21]They all remained standing in place around the camp, while the whole camp began to run and shout and flee. [22]When they blew the three hundred horns, the LORD set the sword of one against another throughout the camp, and they fled as far as Beth-shittah in the direction of Zeredah, near the border of Abel-meholah at Tabbath.

[23]The Israelites were called to arms from Naphtali, from Asher, and from all Manasseh, and they pursued Midian. [24]Gideon also sent messengers throughout the mountain region of Ephraim to say, "Go down to intercept Midian, and seize the water courses against them as far as Beth-barah, as well as the Jordan." So all the Ephraimites were called to arms, and they seized the water courses as far as Beth-barah, and the Jordan as

well. [25]They captured the two princes of Midian, Oreb and Zeeb, killing Oreb at the rock of Oreb and Zeeb at the wine press of Zeeb. Then they pursued Midian, but they had the heads of Oreb and Zeeb brought to Gideon beyond the Jordan.

8 [1]But the Ephraimites said to him, "What have you done to us, not summoning us when you went to fight against Midian?" And they quarreled bitterly with him. [2]But he answered them, "What have I done in comparison with you? Is not the gleaning of Ephraim better than the vintage of Abiezer? [3]It was into your power God delivered the princes of Midian, Oreb and Zeeb. What have I been able to do in comparison with you?" When he said this, their anger against him subsided.

[4]When Gideon reached the Jordan and crossed it, he and his three hundred men were exhausted and famished. [5]So

---

military engagement at all. The noise level created confusion and self-destruction (7:16-22). The scene is reminiscent of Jericho, a prior victory without military engagement (Josh 6). In pursuit of the fleeing enemy, Israel now had the upper hand. With their water supply cut off, the Midianites were vanquished and their two princes beheaded. The recall of Israel's tribal force is historically unlikely (7:23-24); it was a way of again adjusting the numbers after the victory of the three hundred in order to present the victory as accomplished by a united Israel. This was clearly a triumph for Gideon, but more so for the Lord.

8:1-22 The Midianite kings and idolatry

Varied and disconnected narratives are here linked together in bringing the Midianite threat to an end. The similarities between the two kings of this chapter and the two princes formerly mentioned (7:25) may point to parallel traditions regarding the same persons. Here a number of accounts are connected: discussion with the Ephraimites (8:1-3), the reproof and reprisal against Succoth and Penuel (8:4-17), and the sentencing of the Midianite kings (8:18-20).

he said to the people of Succoth, "Will you give my followers some loaves of bread? They are exhausted, and I am pursuing Zebah and Zalmunna, kings of Midian." ⁶But the princes of Succoth replied, "Are the hands of Zebah and Zalmunna already in your possession, that we should give food to your army?" ⁷Gideon said, "Very well; when the LORD has delivered Zebah and Zalmunna into my power, I will thrash your bodies with desert thorns and briers." ⁸He went up from there to Penuel and made the same request of them, but the people of Penuel answered him as had the people of Succoth. ⁹So to the people of Penuel, too, he said, "When I return in peace, I will demolish this tower."

¹⁰Now Zebah and Zalmunna were in Karkor with their force of about fifteen thousand men; these were all who were left of the whole Kedemite army, a hundred and twenty thousand swordsmen having fallen. ¹¹Gideon went up by the route of the tent-dwellers east of Nobah and Jogbehah, and attacked the force when it felt secure. ¹²Zebah and Zalmunna

fled and Gideon pursued them. He captured the two kings of Midian, Zebah and Zalmunna, terrifying the entire force.

¹³Then Gideon, son of Joash, returned from battle by the pass of Heres. ¹⁴He captured a young man of Succoth and questioned him, and he wrote down for him the seventy-seven princes and elders of Succoth. ¹⁵So he went to the princes of Succoth and said, "Here are Zebah and Zalmunna, with whom you taunted me, 'Are the hands of Zebah and Zalmunna already in your possession, that we should give food to your weary men?'" ¹⁶He seized the elders of the city, and with desert thorns and briers he thrashed the people of Succoth. ¹⁷He also demolished the tower of Penuel and killed the people of the city.

¹⁸Then he said to Zebah and Zalmunna, "What about the men you killed at Tabor?" "They were all like you," they replied. "They appeared to be princes." ¹⁹"They were my brothers, my mother's sons," he said. "As the LORD lives, if you had spared their lives, I would not kill you." ²⁰Then he said to his firstborn,

---

The discussion with Ephraim underscores that tribe's importance and the need for consultation when any action was taken in that region. There were, however, advantages for Ephraim to be obtained out of the conflict, as indicated in the adage (8:2). War had been waged by the Abiezerites, but the Ephraimities gleaned the fruits of victory; it was the latter who had captured the enemy princes (7:24-27).

The dealings with Succoth and Penuel in Transjordan find these settlements hostile and arrogant (8:4-12). Food was to be given only with the removal of the threat (8:6). When Gideon captured the fleeing kings at Karkor, an unidentified location east of the Jordan and a Midianite attack point, he returned to Succoth and Penuel and inflicted severe penalties on the city leaders and the male population, notwithstanding the fact that they were part of the Israelite population (8:13-17). The point of this and the

Jether, "Go, kill them." But the boy did not draw his sword, for he was afraid, for he was still a boy. ²¹ Zebah and Zalmunna said, "Come, kill us yourself, for as a man is, so is his strength." So Gideon stepped forward and killed Zebah and Zalmunna. He also took the crescents that were on the necks of their camels.

²² The Israelites then said to Gideon, "Rule over us—you, your son, and your son's son—for you saved us from the power of Midian." ²³But Gideon answered them, "I will not rule over you, nor shall my son rule over you. The LORD must rule over you."

²⁴Gideon went on to say, "Let me make a request of you. Give me, each of you, a ring from his spoils." (Since they were Ishmaelites, the enemy had gold rings.) ²⁵"We will certainly give them," they replied, and they spread out a cloak into which everyone threw a ring from his spoils. ²⁶The gold rings he had requested weighed seventeen hundred gold shekels, apart from the crescents and pendants, the purple garments worn by the kings of Midian, and apart from the trappings that were on the necks of their camels. ²⁷Gideon made an ephod out of the gold and placed it in his city, Ophrah. All Israel prostituted themselves there, and it became a snare to Gideon and his household.

²⁸Midian was brought into subjection by the Israelites; they no longer held their heads high, and the land had rest for forty years, during the lifetime of Gideon.

Gideon's Son Abimelech. ²⁹Then Jerubbaal, son of Joash, went to live in his house. ³⁰Now Gideon had seventy sons, his own offspring, for he had many wives. ³¹His concubine who lived in Shechem also bore him a son, whom he named Abimelech. ³²At a good old age Gideon, son of Joash, died and was buried in the tomb of Joash his father in Ophrah of the Abiezrites. ³³But after Gideon was dead, the Israelites again prostituted themselves by following the Baals, making Baal-berith their god. ³⁴The Israelites did not remember the LORD, their God, who had delivered them from the power of their enemies all around them. ³⁵Nor were they loyal to the house of Jerubbaal (Gideon) for all the good he had done for Israel.

Ephraim account underscores the importance of Israel's acting in concert in the face of a threat, brooking no opposition.

The death of the two kings is said to be in reprisal for the death of Gideon's brothers, about which we have been told nothing (8:18-21). Such a vendetta would have been customary, however, in keeping with the law of retribution (Deut 19:21; Lev 24:17). The only concession made was that the execution was carried out by Gideon and not his inexperienced son.

8:22-29 The death of Gideon

This is the earliest mention of kingship and its tone is clearly anti-monarchical (8:22-23). This train of thought will emerge strongly in the time of Samuel (1 Sam 8). An earthly kingship inevitably compromised the singular sovereignty which belonged to YHWH.

9 ¹Abimelech, son of Jerubbaal, went to his mother's kin in Shechem, and said to them and to the whole clan to which his mother's family belonged, ²"Put this question to all the lords of Shechem: 'Which is better for you: that seventy men, all Jerubbaal's sons, rule over you, or that one man rule over you?' You must remember that I am your own flesh and bone." ³When his mother's kin repeated these words on his behalf to all the lords of Shechem, they set their hearts on Abimelech, thinking, "He is our kin." ⁴They also gave him seventy pieces of silver from the temple of Baal-berith, with which Abimelech hired worthless men and outlaws as his followers. ⁵He then went to his father's house in Ophrah, and killed his brothers, the seventy sons of Jerubbaal, on one stone. Only the young-est son of Jerubbaal, Jotham, escaped, for he was hidden. ⁶Then all the lords of Shechem and all Beth-millo came together and made Abimelech king by the tere-binth at the memorial pillar in Shechem.

⁷When this was reported to Jotham, he went and stood at the top of Mount Gerizim and cried out in a loud voice:

"Hear me, lords of Shechem,
    and may God hear you!
⁸One day the trees went out
    to anoint a king over themselves.
So they said to the olive tree,
    'Reign over us.'
⁹But the olive tree answered them,
    'Must I give up my rich oil,
    whereby gods and human beings
        are honored,
    and go off to hold sway over the
        trees?'

Unfortunately Gideon turns to idolatry, bringing his story to a disap-pointing end (8:24-27). Midianites and Ishmaelites were interchangeable, both finding their origins in nomadic tribes (8:24; cf. Gen 37:25-28). Out of the gold collected, Gideon made a cult object. The ephod (8:27) was part of the priestly attire (1 Sam 2:18) but was also an instrument for discerning the divine will (1 Sam 14:3, 18-19). In Judges, it is connected with idols (17:5; 18:14), which is its obvious meaning here. It leads to the ruin of Gideon and his family. This unfortunate event notwithstanding, the Deuteronomist's cycle ends with a forty-year peace (8:28).

The chapter's ending attempts to bring the Gideon and Jerubbaal tradi-tions together (8:29-32). It is Jerubbaal's son who will come to the fore in the next chapter. Noted again is the Israelite's reversion to former idolatrous practices in honor of Baal-berith (the lord of the covenant) after the death of Gideon.

9:1-56 The reign of Abimelech

The chapter views Israel's first experience of kingship in a very negative light. It contains Abimelech's bid for the throne (9:1-6), the prophetic op-position of his brother Jotham (9:7-21), the battle at Shechem (9:22-45) and Migdal-shechem (9:46-49), and the death of Abimelech (9:50-56).

¹⁰Then the trees said to the fig tree,
'Come; you reign over us!'
¹¹But the fig tree answered them,
'Must I give up my sweetness
and my sweet fruit,
and go off to hold sway over the
trees?'
¹²Then the trees said to the vine,
'Come you, reign over us.'
¹³But the vine answered them,
'Must I give up my wine
that cheers gods and human
beings,
and go off to hold sway over the
trees?'
¹⁴Then all the trees said to the
buckthorn,
'Come; you reign over us!'
¹⁵The buckthorn answered the trees,
'If you are anointing me in good
faith,
to make me king over you,
come, and take refuge in my
shadow.

But if not, let fire come from the
buckthorn
and devour the cedars of
Lebanon.'

¹⁶"Now then, if you have acted in good faith and integrity in appointing Abimelech your king, if you have acted with good will toward Jerubbaal and his house, and if you have treated him as he deserved— ¹⁷for my father fought for you at the risk of his life when he delivered you from the power of Midian, ¹⁸but you have risen against my father's house today and killed his seventy sons upon one stone and made Abimelech, the son of his maidservant, king over the lords of Shechem, because he is your kin— ¹⁹if, then, you have acted in good faith and integrity toward Jerubbaal and his house today, then rejoice in Abimelech and may he in turn rejoice in you! ²⁰But if not, let fire come forth from Abimelech and

---

Abimelech, son of Jerubbaal, made an ambitious appeal for the throne in Israel before his maternal relatives at Shechem, claiming preference over the other sixty-nine sons of Jerubbaal. With his end in sight, he eliminated any possible opposition by killing his brothers, with the exception of one, the young Jotham. He attained his goal and was proclaimed king at Shechem (9:1-6).

Jotham's presentation of the choice in figurative and poetic language cannot conceal the obvious conclusion. The selection would be based not on quality but political greed and inferior ambition. In choosing Abimelech, a man guilty of fratricide, they would have a king amounting to little more than the common buckthorn plant (9:7-12). In Jotham's warning, there is a clear indication of Shechem's destruction by the king (9:20).

The people's eventual disenchantment with their king found them receptive to the revolutionary overture of Gaal (9:22-29). However, the king retained an ally in the city in the person of Zebul (9:30-33). The revolt proved unsuccessful and Gaal's forces were defeated in a pitched battle (9:34-41); Abimelech then took the city of Shechem by ambushing the local population

devour the lords of Shechem and Beth-millo, and let fire come forth from the lords of Shechem and Beth-millo and devour Abimelech." ²¹Then Jotham fled and escaped to Beer, where he remained for fear of his brother Abimelech.

²²When Abimelech had ruled Israel for three years, ²³God put an evil spirit between Abimelech and the lords of Shechem, and the lords of Shechem broke faith with the house of Abimelech. ²⁴This was to repay the violence done to the seventy sons of Jerubbaal and to avenge their blood upon their brother Abimelech, who killed them, and upon the lords of Shechem, who encouraged him to kill his brothers. ²⁵The lords of Shechem then set men in ambush for him on the mountaintops, and they robbed all who passed them on the road. It was reported to Abimelech.

²⁶Now Gaal, son of Ebed, and his kin came, and when they passed through Shechem, the lords of Shechem put their trust in him. ²⁷They went out into the fields, harvested the grapes from their vineyards, trod them out, and held a festival. Then they went to the temple of their god, where they ate and drank and cursed Abimelech. ²⁸Gaal, son of Ebed, said, "Who is Abimelech? And who is Shechem that we should serve him? Did not the son of Jerubbaal and his lieuten-

ant Zebul serve the men of Hamor, father of Shechem? So why should we serve him? ²⁹Would that these troops were entrusted to my command! I would depose Abimelech. I would say to Abimelech, 'Get a larger army and come out!'"

³⁰When Zebul, the ruler of the city, heard what Gaal, son of Ebed, had said, he was angry ³¹and sent messengers to Abimelech in Arumah to say, "Gaal, son of Ebed, and his kin have come to Shechem and are stirring up the city against you. ³²So take action tonight, you and the troops who are with you, and set an ambush in the fields. ³³Promptly at sunrise tomorrow morning, make a raid on the city. When he and the troops who are with him come out against you, deal with him as best you can."

³⁴During the night Abimelech went into action with all his soldiers and set up an ambush outside of Shechem in four companies. ³⁵Gaal, son of Ebed, went out and stood at the entrance of the city gate. When Abimelech and his soldiers rose from their place of ambush, ³⁶Gaal saw the soldiers and said to Zebul, "There are soldiers coming down from the mountaintops!" But Zebul answered him, "It is the shadow of the hills that you see as men." ³⁷But Gaal went on to say, "Soldiers are coming down from the region of Tabbur-haarez, and one

---

(9:42-45). "[S]owing it with salt" (9:45) remains unclear, except for the fact that a salted earth was a symbol of devastation (Jer 17:6)

Another source speaks of the tragedy of the Tower of Shechem (*Migdal-Shechem*; 9:46-49). Ironically the people were killed during idolatrous worship of the pagan god of the covenant (9:46; 8:33). Abimelech had completed his task, and the prophecy of Jotham was fulfilled. The Shechemites were put to the torch by the buckthorn (9:13, 20).

company is coming by way of Elon-meonenim." ³⁸Zebul said to him, "Where now is your boast, when you said, 'Who is Abimelech that we should serve him?' Are these not the troops for whom you expressed contempt? Go out now and fight with them." ³⁹So Gaal went out at the head of the lords of Shechem to fight against Abimelech; ⁴⁰but when Abimelech went after him, he fled from him. Many fell slain right up to the entrance of the gate. ⁴¹Abimelech returned to Arumah, and Zebul drove Gaal and his kin away so that they could no longer remain at Shechem.

⁴²The next day, the army marched out into the field, and it was reported to Abimelech. ⁴³He divided the troops he had into three companies, and set up an ambush in the fields. He watched until he saw the army leave the city and then went on the attack against them. ⁴⁴Abimelech and the company with him rushed in and stood by the entrance of the city gate, while the other two companies rushed upon all who were in the field and attacked them. ⁴⁵That entire day Abimelech fought against the city. He captured it, killed the people who were in it, and demolished the city itself, sowing it with salt.

⁴⁶When they heard of this, all the lords of the Migdal-shechem went into the crypt of the temple of El-berith. ⁴⁷It was reported to Abimelech that all the lords of the Migdal-shechem were gathered together. ⁴⁸So he went up Mount Zalmon with all his soldiers, took his ax in his hand, and cut down some brushwood. This he lifted to his shoulder, then said to the troops with him, "Hurry! Do just as you have seen me do." ⁴⁹So all the soldiers likewise cut down brushwood and, following Abimelech, placed it against the crypt. Then they set the crypt on fire over them, so that every one of the people of the Migdal-shechem, about a thousand men and women, perished.

⁵⁰Abimelech proceeded to Thebez, encamped, and captured it. ⁵¹Now there was a strong tower in the middle of the city, and all the men and women and all the lords of the city fled there, shutting themselves in and going up to the roof of the tower. ⁵²Abimelech came up to the tower and fought against it. When he came close to the entrance of the tower to set it on fire, ⁵³a certain woman cast the upper part of a millstone down on Abimelech's head, and it fractured his skull. ⁵⁴He immediately called his armor-bearer and said to him, "Draw your sword and put me to death so they will not say about me, 'A woman killed him.'" So his attendant ran him through and he died. ⁵⁵When the Israelites saw that Abimelech was dead, they all left for their homes.

⁵⁶Thus did God repay the evil that Abimelech had done to his father in killing his seventy brothers. ⁵⁷God also brought all the wickedness of the people of Shechem back on their heads, for the

---

There is incredible irony in the death of Abimelech at Thebez, an unknown location, identified by some with modern Tubas. He was killed by a falling stone thrown by a woman (9:50-55). In ordering his armor bearer to dispatch him, he was assured that his death will be given a more honored place in history. With this tragedy, the beginnings of kingship were brought

curse of Jotham, son of Jerubbaal, overtook them.

10 **Tola.** ¹After Abimelech, Tola, son of Puah, son of Dodo, a man of Issachar, rose up to save Israel; he lived in Shamir in the mountain region of Ephraim. ²When he had judged Israel twenty-three years, he died and was buried in Shamir.

Jair. ³Jair the Gileadite came after him and judged Israel twenty-two years. ⁴He had thirty sons who rode on thirty donkeys and possessed thirty cities in the land of Gilead (these are called Havvoth-jair to the present day). ⁵Jair died and was buried in Kamon.

Oppression by the Ammonites. ⁶The Israelites again did what was evil in the sight of the LORD, serving the Baals and Ashtarts, the gods of Aram, the gods of Sidon, the gods of Moab, the gods of the Ammonites, and the gods of the Philistines. Since they had abandoned the LORD and would not serve him, ⁷the LORD became angry with Israel and he sold them into the power of the Philistines and the Ammonites. ⁸For eighteen years they afflicted and oppressed the Israelites in Bashan, and all the Israelites in the Amorite land beyond the Jordan in Gilead. ⁹The Ammonites also crossed the Jordan to fight against Judah, Benjamin and the house of Ephraim, so that Israel was in great distress.

¹⁰Then the Israelites cried out to the LORD, "We have sinned against you, for we have abandoned our God and served the Baals." ¹¹The LORD answered the Israelites: Did not the Egyptians, the Amorites, the Ammonites, the Philistines, ¹²the Sidonians, the Amalekites, and the Midianites oppress you? Yet when you cried out to me, and I saved you from their power, ¹³you still abandoned me and served other gods. Therefore I will save you no more. ¹⁴Go and cry out to the gods you have chosen; let them save you in your time of distress. ¹⁵But the Israelites said to the LORD, "We have sinned. Do to us whatever is good in your sight. Only deliver us this day!" ¹⁶And they cast out the foreign gods

---

to a bitter end. For the Deuteronomist it was due retribution for a fratricidal king and an unfaithful population (9:56).

10:1-5 Minor judges

Passing reference is made to two judges, Tola of Issachar and Jair of Gilead, who "judged" Israel for twenty-three and twenty-two years respectively. Jair was a man of means (who possessed saddle asses, cf. Judg 5:10). The mention of the two of them in a climate of peace and harmony contrasts with the turmoil of Abimelech's reign. The absence of any mention of military undertakings points to the broader understanding of "judgeship" in the sense of leadership.

10:6-17 Ammonite oppression

The Deuteronomistic framework reappears forcefully in this prelude to the story of Jephthah, and, more broadly, to the second part of the book.

from their midst and served the LORD, so that he grieved over the misery of Israel.

¹⁷The Ammonites were called out for war and encamped in Gilead, while the Israelites assembled and encamped at Mizpah. ¹⁸The captains of the army of Gilead said to one another, "The one who begins the war against the Ammonites shall be leader of all the inhabitants of Gilead."

11 **Jephthah.** ¹Jephthah the Gileadite was a warrior. He was the son of a prostitute, fathered by Gilead. ²Gilead's wife had also borne him sons. When they grew up the sons of the wife had driven Jephthah away, saying to him, "You shall inherit nothing in our father's house, for you are the son of another woman." ³So Jephthah had fled from his brothers and taken up residence in the land of Tob. Worthless men had joined company with him, and went out with him on raids.

⁴Some time later, the Ammonites went to war with Israel. ⁵As soon as the Ammonites were at war with Israel, the elders of Gilead went to bring Jephthah from the land of Tob. ⁶"Come," they said to Jephthah, "be our commander so that we can fight the Ammonites." ⁷"Are you not the ones who hated me and drove me from my father's house?" Jephthah replied to the elders of Gilead, "Why do you come to me now, when you are in distress?" ⁸The elders of Gilead said to Jephthah, "This is the reason we have come back to you now: if you go with us to fight against the Ammonites, you shall be the leader of all of the inhabitants of Gilead." ⁹Jephthah answered the

There is the reference to idolatry (10:6), punishment (10:7-9), and repentance (10:10). There is specific reference to the Ammonite incursion east and west of the Jordan, an appropriate introduction to the role of Jephthah (10:8-9). Moreover, the repentance of the Israelites is here more detailed, with a twofold plea to the Lord (10:10, 15) and concrete steps to eliminate idolatry (10:16). With hostilities running high, the opposing forces prepare for battle (10:17-18). The chapter ends with a prophetic allusion to the forthcoming role of Jephthah.

11:1-40 Jephthah

The tribes of Gad and Manasseh occupied the region of Gilead in Transjordan. Jephthah, whose birth was illegitimate, was a native of the region, the son of a man bearing the region's name. His father's other sons disowned their half-brother because of his illegitimate origins; distanced from his home, Jephthah joined ranks with a band of brigands (11:1-3).

At this point, the family of the man named Gilead merges with the Gileadite tribes. Thus, it is the elders of Gilead whom Jephthah accuses of driving him from his father's house. Jephthah is seen as a credible warrior. He assumed leadership to wage war against Ammon, with his future position secure (11:9-10).

elders of Gilead, "If you bring me back to fight against the Ammonites and the LORD delivers them up to me, I will be your leader." ¹⁰The elders of Gilead said to Jephthah, "The LORD is witness between us that we will do as you say." ¹¹So Jephthah went with the elders of Gilead, and the army made him their leader and commander. Jephthah gave all his orders in the presence of the LORD in Mizpah.

¹²Then he sent messengers to the king of the Ammonites to say, "What do you have against me that you come to fight with me in my land?" ¹³The king of the Ammonites answered the messengers of Jephthah, "Israel took away my land from the Arnon to the Jabbok and the Jordan when they came up from Egypt. Now restore it peaceably."

¹⁴Again Jephthah sent messengers to the king of the Ammonites, ¹⁵saying to him, "This is what Jephthah says: 'Israel did not take the land of Moab or the land of the Ammonites. ¹⁶For when they came up from Egypt, Israel went through the wilderness to the Red Sea and came to Kadesh. ¹⁷Israel then sent messengers to the king of Edom saying, "Let me pass through your land." But the king of Edom did not give consent. They also sent to the king of Moab, but he too was unwilling. So Israel remained in Kadesh. ¹⁸Then they went through the wilderness, and bypassing the land of Edom and the land of Moab, they arrived east of the land of Moab and encamped across the Arnon. Thus they did not enter the territory of Moab, for the Arnon is the boundary of Moab. ¹⁹Then Israel sent messengers to the Amorite king Sihon, who was king of Heshbon. Israel said to him, "Let me pass through your land to my own place." ²⁰But Sihon refused to let Israel pass through his territory. He gathered all his soldiers, and they encamped at Jahaz and fought Israel. ²¹But the LORD, the God of Israel, delivered Sihon and his entire army into the power of Israel, who defeated them and occupied all the land of the Amorites who lived in that region. ²²They occupied all of the Amorite territory from the Arnon to the Jabbok and the wilderness to the Jordan. ²³Now, then, it was the LORD, the God of Israel, who dispossessed the Amorites for his people, Israel. And you are going to dispossess them? ²⁴Should you not take possession of that which your god Chemosh gave you to possess, and should we not take possession of all that the LORD, our God, has dispossessed for us? ²⁵Now, then, are you any better than Balak, son of Zippor, king of Moab? Did he ever quarrel with

---

The new judge's first ploy was diplomatic, sending a delegation to the king of Ammon. After first obtaining the Lord's assurance (11:11), he learned of Ammonite intentions in the Transjordan to "repossess" the land lying between the Arnon and Jabbok rivers (11:11-13). Jephthah rejected the demand through a second delegation, illustrating the legitimacy of Israel's claim. The account of Israel's dealings in the past with Moab, Edom, and the Amorites is in basic agreement with the Pentateuchal narrative found in Numbers 20–24. The disputed territory, now occupied by the Israelites in the Transjordan, had been taken in the war against the Amorites; Israel's

Israel or make war against them? [26]Israel has dwelt in Heshbon and its villages, Aroer and its villages, and all the cities on the banks of the Arnon for three hundred years. Why did you not recover them during that time? [27]As for me, I have not sinned against you, but you wrong me by making war against me. Let the LORD, who is judge, decide this day between the Israelites and the Ammonites!'" [28]But the king of the Ammonites paid no heed to the message Jephthah sent him.

Jephthah's Vow. [29]The spirit of the LORD came upon Jephthah. He passed through Gilead and Manasseh, and through Mizpah of Gilead as well, and from Mizpah of Gilead he crossed over against the Ammonites. [30]Jephthah made a vow to the LORD. "If you deliver the Ammonites into my power," he said, [31]"whoever comes out of the doors of my house to meet me when I return from the Ammonites in peace shall belong to the LORD. I shall offer him up as a burnt offering."

[32]Jephthah then crossed over against the Ammonites to fight against them, and the LORD delivered them into his power. [33]He inflicted a very severe defeat on them from Aroer to the approach of Minnith—twenty cities in all—and as far as Abel-keramin. So the Ammonites were brought into subjection by the Israelites. [34]When Jephthah returned to his house in Mizpah, it was his daughter who came out to meet him, with tambourine-playing and dancing. She was his only child: he had neither son nor daughter besides her. [35]When he saw her, he tore his garments and said, "Ah, my daughter! You have struck me down and brought calamity upon me. For I have made a vow to the LORD and I cannot take it back." [36]"Father," she replied, "you have made a vow to the LORD. Do with me as you have vowed, because the LORD has taken vengeance for you against your enemies the Ammonites." [37]Then she said to her father, "Let me have this favor. Do nothing for two months, that I and my companions may go wander in the mountains to weep for my virginity." [38]"Go," he replied, and sent her away for two months. So she departed with her companions and wept

---

claim is legitimate. Since Ammon's designs on westward expansion had been thwarted, war was seen as the only solution. In holding that each country's god establishes boundaries, Jephthah is speaking in diplomatic, not theological, terms (11:24). Either the author or a later copyist has confused the god of the Moabites, Chemosh, with the god of the Ammonites, Molech (cf. Num 21:29; 1 Kgs 11:7). But Jephthah's voice fell on deaf ears. War was now inevitable (11:28).

That the spirit of the Lord has empowered Jephthah does not suffice. He further makes a vow to the Lord in what may have originally been a separate and isolated incident. In exchange for victory, he will sacrifice the first person to emerge from his house upon his return (11:29-31). Human sacrifice was not uncommon among Israel's pagan neighbors but was not

for her virginity in the mountains. ³⁹At the end of the two months she returned to her father, and he did to her as he had vowed. She had not had relations with any man.

It became a custom in Israel ⁴⁰for Israelite women to go yearly to mourn the daughter of Jephthah the Gileadite for four days of the year.

12 The Shibboleth Incident. ¹The men of Ephraim were called out, and they crossed over to Zaphon. They said to Jephthah, "Why did you go to fight with the Ammonites without calling us to go with you? We will burn your house on top of you." ²Jephthah answered them, "My soldiers and I were engaged in a contest with the Ammonites. They were pressing us hard, and I cried out to you, but you did not come to save me from their power. ³When I saw that you were not coming to save me, I took my life in my own hand and crossed over against the Ammonites, and the LORD delivered them into my power. Why, then, should you come up against me this day to fight with me?"

⁴Then Jephthah gathered together all the men of Gilead and fought against Ephraim. The men of Gilead defeated Ephraim, ⁵and Gilead seized the fords of the Jordan against Ephraim. When any of the fleeing Ephraimites said, "Let me pass," the men of Gilead would say to him, "Are you an Ephraimite?" If he answered, "No!" ⁶they would ask him to say "Shibboleth." If he said "Sibboleth," not pronouncing it exactly right, they would seize him and kill him at the fords of the Jordan. Forty-two thousand Ephraimites fell at that time.

⁷Jephthah judged Israel for six years, and Jephthah the Gileadite died and was buried in his city in Gilead.

---

practiced in Israel (Lev 18:21; 20:2-5; Deut 12:31; Mic 6:7). The possibility of its limited toleration in early pre-monarchical times cannot be categorically ruled out. Here the author passes no judgment on Jephthah's decision; it was secondary to the vow itself, which had to be upheld at all cost.

The Ammonites were defeated. The vow was fulfilled even though it meant the sacrifice of Jephthah's only child. That she was a virgin and therefore childless was cause for mourning in itself. This was an unwanted fate for any Israelite woman and called for a period of mourning. For this the daughter was granted a two-month reprieve (11:32-39). The final verse indicates that this may have been written to explain a local annual mourning ritual (11:40).

12:1-7 Internal conflict

The civil conflict between Gilead and Ephraim may have been originally unrelated to Jephthah. It is inserted here to complement his position as a major judge. A contentious Ephraim has appeared before (12:1, cf. 8:1). The confrontation with Jephthah took place at Zaphon in Gileadite territory. The account reflects the uneasiness of tribal isolation in the absence of any national unity, clearly seen in the case of the insurgent Abimelech in chapter

Ibzan. [8]After him Ibzan of Bethlehem judged Israel. [9]He had thirty sons and thirty daughters whom he gave in marriage outside the family, while bringing in thirty wives for his sons from outside the family. He judged Israel for seven years. [10]Ibzan died and was buried in Bethlehem.

Elon. [11]After him Elon the Zebulunite judged Israel; he judged Israel for ten years. [12]Elon the Zebulunite died and was buried at Aijalon in the land of Zebulun.

Abdon. [13]After him Abdon, son of Hillel, the Pirathonite, judged Israel. [14]He had forty sons and thirty grandsons, who rode on seventy donkeys. He judged Israel for eight years. [15]Abdon, son of Hillel, the Pirathonite, died and was buried in Pirathon in the land of Ephraim in the mountain region of the Amalekites.

13 The Birth of Samson. [1]The Israelites again did what was evil in the sight of the LORD, who therefore

---

9. There would seem to be an indication here of Ephraim's intent to move beyond the Jordan, insinuating a claim to territory there (12:4). The charismatic Jephthah and his forces thwarted them. Differences in pronunciation between Ephraimites and Gileadites afforded the opportunity to unmask the fleeing Ephraimites and put them to death (12:6). After a relatively short judgeship, Jephthah died and was buried in his native city (12:7).

12:8-13 More minor judges

Elon and Abdon were from Zebulun and Ephraim respectively. Abdon was from Pirathon on the Ephraim–Manasseh border. Ibzan is identified with Bethlehem, which many authors see as the northern town in Zebulon not the more familiar Bethlehem of Judah. Once again, the judges here seem to have had administrative functions. They ruled after the death of Jephthah in a twenty-five year period marked by peace and harmony.

13:1–16:31 Samson

Referred to by one biblical scholar as a "wenching lout," Samson is one of the most enigmatic persons in the Bible. The accounts of his life have the aura of legend and folklore. Rather than a person raised up as a judge to liberate his people, his exploits seem to be more personal in character, underscoring his personal prowess or vindicating his own position. In this he differs from the other judges. His personal life leaves much to be desired—rash responses, lust for women, disregard of his vowed status. Yet it is in his weakness that the power of YHWH appears most strongly. In Samson the Lord often triumphs not because of him but in spite of him. The narrative comes from a variety of independent sources and is divided: birth (13:1-24), marriage to a Philistine (14:1-9), Philistine defeat (15:1-20), prostitute encounter (16:1-3), Delilah (16:4-22), and finally death (16:23-31).

delivered them into the power of the Philistines for forty years.

²There was a certain man from Zorah, of the clan of the Danites, whose name was Manoah. His wife was barren and had borne no children. ³An angel of the LORD appeared to the woman and said to her: Though you are barren and have had no children, you will conceive and bear a son. ⁴Now, then, be careful to drink no wine or beer and to eat nothing unclean, ⁵for you will conceive and bear a son. No razor shall touch his head, for the boy is to be a nazirite for God from the womb. It is he who will begin to save Israel from the power of the Philistines.

⁶The woman went and told her husband, "A man of God came to me; he had the appearance of an angel of God, fearsome indeed. I did not ask him where he came from, nor did he tell me his name. ⁷But he said to me, 'You will conceive and bear a son. So drink no wine or beer, and eat nothing unclean. For the boy shall be a nazirite for God from the womb, until the day of his death.'" ⁸Manoah then prayed to the LORD. "Please, my Lord," he said, "may the man of God whom you sent return to us to teach us what to do for the boy who is to be born."

⁹God heard the prayer of Manoah, and the angel of God came again to the woman as she was sitting in the field; but her husband Manoah was not with her. ¹⁰The woman ran quickly and told her husband. "The man who came to me the other day has appeared to me," she said to him; ¹¹so Manoah got up and followed his wife. When he reached the man, he said to him, "Are you the one who spoke to my wife?" I am, he answered. ¹²Then Manoah asked, "Now, when what you say comes true, what rules must the boy follow? What must he do?" ¹³The angel of the LORD answered Manoah: Your wife must be careful about all the things of which I spoke to her. ¹⁴She must not eat anything that comes from the vine, she must not drink wine or beer, and she must not eat anything unclean. Let her observe all that I have commanded her. ¹⁵Then Manoah said to the angel of the LORD, "Permit us to detain you, so that we may prepare a young goat for you." ¹⁶But the angel of

13:1-24 Birth

The Philistines occupied the coastal region of central Canaan in the twelfth century B.C., close to the time of the Israelite occupation of the land. Formerly in Judges, the enemy threat came principally from the east; here it lies to the west. In Samson's time the Philistines dominated the central part of the country (13:1). Samson's father, Manoah, was a Danite from Zorah in the south, a town which had been allotted to Dan (Josh 19:4); this was before the migration of the tribe north, leaving Zorah as part of Judah (Josh 15:33).

There are several accounts of the announcement of important births in the Old Testament, e.g., Isaac (Gen 15:1-6) and Samuel (1 Sam 1). Here the angel of the Lord is a visible manifestation of YHWH himself (13:21-22). The exceptional character of the forthcoming birth is clear: the barren wife

the LORD answered Manoah: Though you detained me, I would not eat your food. But if you want to prepare a burnt offering, then offer it up to the LORD. For Manoah did not know that he was the angel of the LORD. ¹⁷Then Manoah said to the angel of the LORD, "What is your name, that we may honor you when your words come true?" ¹⁸The angel of the LORD answered him: Why do you ask my name? It is wondrous. ¹⁹Then Manoah took a young goat with a grain offering and offered it on the rock to the LORD, who works wonders. While Manoah and his wife were looking on, ²⁰as the flame rose to the heavens from the altar, the angel of the LORD ascended in the flame of the altar. When Manoah and his wife saw this, they fell on their faces to the ground; ²¹but the angel of the LORD was seen no more by Manoah and

his wife. Then Manoah, realizing that it was the angel of the LORD, ²²said to his wife, "We will certainly die, for we have seen God." ²³But his wife said to him, "If the LORD had meant to kill us, he would not have accepted a burnt offering and grain offering from our hands! Nor would he have let us see all this, or hear what we have heard."

²⁴The woman bore a son and named him Samson, and when the boy grew up the LORD blessed him. ²⁵The spirit of the LORD came upon him for the first time in Mahaneh-dan, between Zorah and Eshtaol.

14 **Marriage of Samson.** ¹Samson went down to Timnah where he saw one of the Philistine women. ²On his return he told his father and mother, "I saw in Timnah a woman, a Philistine. Get her for me as a wife." ³His father and

---

conceives by divine design (13:3), and Nazirite features are connected with his birth (13:4-5; see Num 6:2-8). The law of abstinence is imposed on the child's mother and his hair is not to be cut. These are external features of his consecration to the Lord (13:5b).

Solemnity is added through the double announcement, first to the mother (13:3-7) and then the father (13:13-14). The son's mission will be the liberation of his people, in a departure from the usual formula of this promise following upon a plea for deliverance (13:5). Underscoring the divine character of the vision, the angel vanishes in flame, the holocaust is offered, and there is the refusal of identification (13:17-20). Knowledge of the name gave authority or dominion over the one named and is thus excluded (Gen 2:20; 32:30). Soon after his birth Samson was spirit-empowered and his destiny was fixed (13:25).

14:1-20 Marriage

In the twofold prediction about Samson, he was to be consecrated to the Lord and would initiate deliverance from the Philistines (13:5). The first is highlighted in the circumstances of his birth (13:24-25); the second, in the account of his marriage.

mother said to him, "Is there no woman among your kinsfolk or among all your people, that you must go and take a woman from the uncircumcised Philistines?" But Samson answered his father, "Get her for me, for she is the one I want." ⁴Now his father and mother did not know that this had been brought about by the LORD, who was seeking an opportunity against the Philistines; for at that time they ruled over Israel.

⁵So Samson went down to Timnah with his father and mother. When he turned aside to the vineyards of Timnah, a young lion came roaring out toward him. ⁶But the spirit of the LORD rushed upon Samson, and he tore the lion apart barehanded, as one tears a young goat. Without telling his father or mother what he had done, ⁷he went down and spoke to the woman. He liked her. ⁸Later, when he came back to marry her, he turned aside to look at the remains of the lion, and there was a swarm of bees in the lion's carcass, and honey. ⁹So he scooped the honey out into his hands and ate it as he went along. When he came to his father and mother, he gave them some to eat, but he did not tell them that he had scooped the honey from the lion's carcass.

¹⁰His father also went down to the woman, and Samson gave a feast there, since it was customary for the young men to do this. ¹¹Out of their fear of him, they brought thirty men to be his companions. ¹²Samson said to them, "Let me propose a riddle to you. If within the seven days of the feast you solve it for me, I will give you thirty linen tunics and thirty sets of garments. ¹³But if you cannot answer it for me, you must give me thirty tunics and thirty sets of garments." "Propose your riddle," they responded, "and we will listen to it." ¹⁴So he said to them,

"Out of the eater came food,
out of the strong came
sweetness."

For three days they were unable to answer the riddle, ¹⁵and on the fourth day they said to Samson's wife, "Trick your husband into solving the riddle for us, or we will burn you and your family. Did you invite us here to reduce us to poverty?" ¹⁶So Samson's wife wept at his side and said, "You just hate me! You do

---

Timnah was in Philistine territory but a short distance from Zorah. Samson's impulsive attraction to an unnamed Philistine woman manifested more lust than discernment (14:1-2). His parents' objection to the marriage on religious grounds is overridden by the editorial comment in verse 4: this was God's way of inserting Samson into Philistine life.

The role of the parents in obtaining the girl's hand is confusing. They are said to accompany their son (14:5) and yet are distant from the events described; in fact, there is an allusion to his second trip to marry the girl, wherein the mother and father are mentioned (14:6-9) and subsequently the father alone (14:10). There is evidently here an uneven blending of sources. The slaughter of the lion exemplifies the hero's exceptional strength (14:6),

not love me! You proposed a riddle to my people, but did not tell me the answer." He said to her, "If I did not tell even my father or my mother, must I tell you?" [17]But she wept beside him during the seven days the feast lasted, and on the seventh day, he told her the answer, because she pressed him, and she explained the riddle to her people.

[18]On the seventh day, before the sun set, the men of the city said to him,

"What is sweeter than honey,
what is stronger than a lion?"

He replied to them,

"If you had not plowed with
my heifer,
you would not have solved
my riddle."

[19]The spirit of the LORD rushed upon him, and he went down to Ashkelon, where he killed thirty of their men and stripped them; he gave their garments to those who had answered the riddle. Then he went off to his own family in anger, [20]and Samson's wife was married to the companion who had been his best man.

15 Samson Defeats the Philistines. [1]After some time, in the season of the wheat harvest, Samson visited his wife, bringing a young goat. But when he said, "Let me go into my wife's room," her father would not let him go in. [2]He said, "I thought you hated her, so I gave her to your best man. Her younger sister is better; you may have

and the later presence of bees in the carcass is prelude to the riddle in the subsequent episode (14:8).

Samson's character as a rogue comes to light in the marriage account. Being the sole outsider puts him at a disadvantage in his in-laws' eyes. He is thus presented with thirty male companions, not only as part of the wedding party but also as future companions in a foreign culture (14:11). The riddle proposed by Samson could never have been solved without knowledge of his prior encounter with the lion: sweet food (honey) comes from the predatory beast. Here it serves as a literary device to enhance Samson's superiority. The use of the wife to obtain the solution subtly foreshadows the following Delilah story (14:13-17). Samson alludes to his wife's role in obtaining the solution to his riddle in his retort, which contains its own ribald nuance (14:18).

Samson has lost his bet but resorts to slaughter to make good on his promise. Acting impulsively he then annuls his marriage. His attack on the Philistines is cruel and boorish. It serves, however, to highlight his superiority and ability to humiliate his foes, all accomplished in "the spirit of the Lord" (14:19).

15:1-20 Philistine defeat

The chapter contains a number of Samson stories which may well have existed independently. There is no essential inter-relatedness in the loss of

her instead." ³Samson said to him, "This time I am guiltless if I harm the Philistines." ⁴So Samson went and caught three hundred jackals, and turning them tail to tail, he took some torches and tied one between each pair of tails. ⁵He then kindled the torches and set the jackals loose in the standing grain of the Philistines, thus burning both the shocks and standing grain, the vineyards and olive groves.

⁶When the Philistines asked, "Who has done this?" they were told, "Samson, the son-in-law of the Timnite, because his wife was taken and given to his best man." So the Philistines went up and destroyed her and her family by fire. ⁷Samson said to them, "If this is how you act, I will not stop until I have taken revenge on you." ⁸And he struck them hip and thigh—a great slaughter. Then he went down and stayed in a cleft of the crag of Etam.

⁹The Philistines went up and encamped in Judah, deploying themselves against Lehi. ¹⁰When the men of Judah asked, "Why have you come up against us?" they answered, "To take Samson prisoner; to do to him as he has done to us." ¹¹Three thousand men of Judah went down to the cleft of the crag of Etam and said to Samson, "Do you not know that the Philistines are our rulers? Why, then, have you done this to us?" He answered them, "As they have done to me, so have I done to them." ¹²They said to him, "We have come down to bind you and deliver you to the Philistines." Samson said to them, "Swear to me that you will not attack me yourselves." ¹³"No," they replied, "we will only bind you and hand you over to them. We will certainly not kill you." So they bound him with two new ropes and brought him up from the crag. ¹⁴When he reached Lehi, and the Philistines came shouting to meet him, the spirit of the LORD rushed upon him: the ropes around his arms became like flax that is consumed by fire, and his bonds melted away from his hands.

---

his wife (15:1-3), the burning of the fields (15:4-5), the defeat of the Philistines (15:6-7), and the annihilation at Lehi (15:9-19). There are, in fact, a number of incongruities in the editorial attempt to unify these stories, e.g., Samson's return to a repudiated wife, a massive response against the Philistines because of his in-laws' limited action against him, then a later strong reaction against the Philistines on behalf of the same despised relatives. However, in the editing of the final text, these are a series of inter-locking episodes highlighting Samson's prowess and charismatic spirit.

The loss of his wife should have come as no surprise to Samson after he had abandoned her (15:1-2; 14:19-20). In Hebrew law, at least at a later date, he could not have taken her back after remarriage (Deut 24:1-4). Rejecting her younger sister, he plans retaliation not against the families but against the Philistine population (15:3). The use of the foxes for incendiary purposes, with its sudden and unforeseen character, was a guerilla tactic (15:4-6). Violence escalates with the killing of his wife and relatives by

¹⁵Coming upon the fresh jawbone of an ass, he reached out, grasped it, and with it killed a thousand men. ¹⁶Then Samson said,

"With the jawbone of an ass
    I have piled them in a heap;
With the jawbone of an ass
    I have slain a thousand men."

¹⁷As he finished speaking he threw the jawbone from him; and so that place was named Ramath-lehi. ¹⁸Being very thirsty, he cried to the LORD and said, "You have put this great victory into the hand of your servant. Must I now die of thirst and fall into the hands of the uncircumcised?" ¹⁹Then God split the cavity in Lehi, and water issued from it, and Samson drank till his spirit returned and he revived. Hence it is called En-hakkore in Lehi to this day.

²⁰Samson judged Israel for twenty years in the days of the Philistines.

16 ¹Once Samson went to Gaza, where he saw a prostitute and visited her. ²The people of Gaza were told, "Samson has come here," and they surrounded him with an ambush at the city gate all night long. And all the night they waited, saying, "At morning light we will kill him." ³Samson lay there until midnight. Then he rose at midnight, seized the doors of the city gate and the two gateposts, and tore them loose, bar

---

the Philistines (15:6), which then leads Samson to single-handed revenge against a great number of his opponents (15:7-8).

The following episode takes place in Judahite territory, a tribe not thus far involved in the Samson narrative. But Judah was also under Philistine domination (15:11); thus they capitulated readily to the occupiers' demand for Samson's extradition. Judah took no chances against their powerful countryman in sending three thousand men to arrest him (15:11). Taking no action against his own people, Samson surrendered without incident. But before being handed over to his enemy, again empowered by the Lord's spirit and with the jawbone of an ass as a weapon, he dispatched one thousand Philistines (15:12-15). The rhyme in 15:16 causes one to wonder to what extent the jingle has influenced the formation of the narrative.

Two etiologies complete the chapter, both of them connected with local sites. Ramath-lehi ("the heights of the jawbone") and En-hakkore ("the spring of the caller") are connected with the battle and the later slaking of the hero's thirst (15:17-19). The conclusion points to an earlier ending of the Samson story at this point (15:20).

16:1-22 A further adventure and Delilah

What this chapter lacks in moral refinement it supplies in vivid drama. The fateful romance between Samson and Delilah is preceded by a bit of folklore surrounding the protagonist (16:1-3). Samson's amorous visit to Gaza in the heart of enemy territory was ruled more by passion than good

and all. He hoisted them on his shoulders and carried them to the top of the ridge opposite Hebron.

Samson and Delilah. ⁴After that he fell in love with a woman in the Wadi Sorek whose name was Delilah. ⁵The lords of the Philistines came up to her and said, "Trick him and find out where he gets his great strength, and how we may overcome and bind him so as to make him helpless. Then for our part, we will each give you eleven hundred pieces of silver."

⁶So Delilah said to Samson, "Tell me where you get your great strength and how you may be bound so as to be made helpless." ⁷"If they bind me with seven fresh bowstrings that have not dried," Samson answered her, "I shall grow weaker and be like anyone else." ⁸So the lords of the Philistines brought her seven fresh bowstrings that had not dried, and she bound him with them. ⁹She had men lying in wait in the room, and she said to him, "The Philistines are upon you, Samson!" But he snapped the bowstrings as a thread of tow is snapped by a whiff of flame; and his strength remained unexplained.

¹⁰Delilah said to Samson, "You have mocked me and told me lies. Now tell me how you may be bound." ¹¹"If they bind me tight with new ropes, with which no work has been done," he answered her, "I shall grow weaker and be like anyone else." ¹²So Delilah took new ropes and bound him with them. Then she said to him, "The Philistines are upon you, Samson!" For there were men lying in wait in the room. But he snapped the ropes off his arms like thread.

¹³Delilah said to Samson again, "Up to now you have mocked me and told me lies. Tell me how you may be bound." He said to her, "If you weave the seven locks of my hair into the web and fasten them with the pin, I shall grow weaker and be like anyone else." ¹⁴So when he went to bed, Delilah took the seven locks of his hair and wove them into the web, and fastened them with the pin. Then she said, "The Philistines are upon you, Samson!" Awakening from his sleep, he pulled out both the loom and the web.

¹⁵Then she said to him, "How can you say 'I love you' when your heart is not mine? Three times already you have mocked me, and not told me where you get your great strength!" ¹⁶She pressed him continually and pestered him till he was deathly weary of it. ¹⁷So he told her all that was in his heart and said, "No razor has touched my head, for I have been a nazirite for God from my mother's womb. If I am shaved, my strength will leave me, and I shall grow weaker and be like anyone else." ¹⁸When Delilah realized that he had told her all that was in

---

sense. But once again moral weakness is overshadowed by physical prowess as he carries the city gate from Gaza in coastal Philistia to Hebron in eastern Judah! The account is clearly didactic in character: a morally weak but empowered Samson renders his pagan foe inept and ridiculous by carrying off the gates of the city.

Still on Philistine soil, Samson became enamored of Delilah (i.e., "flirtatious"). The theme of the story is enunciated by the enemy: to determine the

his heart, she summoned the lords of the Philistines, saying, "Come up this time, for he has told me all that is in his heart." So the lords of the Philistines came to her and brought the money with them. ¹⁹She put him to sleep on her lap, and called for a man who shaved off the seven locks of his hair. He immediately became helpless, for his strength had left him. ²⁰When she said "The Philistines are upon you, Samson!" he woke from his sleep and thought, "I will go out as I have done time and again and shake myself free." He did not realize that the Lᴏʀᴅ had left him. ²¹But the Philistines seized him and gouged out his eyes. Then they brought him down to Gaza and bound him with bronze fetters, and he was put to grinding grain in the prison. ²²But the hair of his head began to grow as soon as it was shaved.

The Death of Samson. ²³ The lords of the Philistines assembled to offer a great sacrifice to their god Dagon and to cele-brate. They said, "Our god has delivered Samson our enemy into our power." ²⁴When the people saw him, they praised their god. For they said,

> "Our god has delivered into our power
> our enemy, the ravager of our land,
> the one who has multiplied our slain."

²⁵When their spirits were high, they said, "Call Samson that he may amuse us." So they called Samson from the prison, and he provided amusement for them. They made him stand between the columns, ²⁶and Samson said to the attendant who was holding his hand, "Put me where I may touch the columns that support the temple, so that I may lean against them." ²⁷The temple was full of men and women: all the lords of the Philistines were there, and from the roof about three thousand men and women looked on as Samson provided amusement. ²⁸Samson cried out

---

source of this Hebrew's strength (16:5). The threefold attempt by Delilah to obtain the answer strains the reader's willingness to accept the unlikely as much as it carries the drama forward. In a match of wits employed by Samson, Delilah is left without the answer (16:6-14). Persistence crowns her efforts as she finally attains her end; his strength is in his hair (16:15-17). This follows logically from his Nazirite vow which forbade the cutting of hair (13:5). With the secret known and the locks shorn, Samson is rendered powerless. The Nazirite vow at this point has become completely unraveled, since he has presumably already broken the other two prohibitions through contact with corpses and the presumed drinking of wine (cf. 14:10). The wounded hero is blinded and subjected to forced labor. Only the mentioned regrowth of the hair sounds an ominous note (16:22).

16:21-31 The death of Samson

As colorful, and even unsavory, as much of the Samson story is, it serves the Deuteronomist's purpose. Regardless of how dire the situation, a return to the Lord brings deliverance. This is clear in the climax of the narrative.

to the Lord and said, "Lord God, remember me! Strengthen me only this once that I may avenge myself on the Philistines at one blow for my two eyes." [29]Samson grasped the two middle columns on which the temple rested and braced himself against them, one at his right, the other at his left. [30]Then saying, "Let me die with the Philistines!" Samson pushed hard, and the temple fell upon the lords and all the people who were in it. Those he killed by his dying were more than those he had killed during his lifetime.

[31]His kinsmen and all his father's house went down and bore him up for burial in the grave of Manoah his father between Zorah and Eshtaol. He had judged Israel for twenty years.

III. Further Stories of the Tribes of Dan and Benjamin

17 **Micah and the Levite.** [1]There was a man from the mountain region of Ephraim whose name was Micah. [2]He said to his mother, "The eleven hundred pieces of silver that were taken from you, about which you pronounced a curse and even said it in my hearing—I have that silver. I took it. So now I will restore it to you." Then his mother said, "May my son be blessed by the Lord!" [3]When he restored the eleven hundred pieces of silver to his mother, she said, "I consecrate the silver to the Lord from my own hand on behalf of my son to make an idol overlaid with silver." [4]So when he restored the silver to his mother, she took two hundred pieces

In the pagan temple to the god Dagon, the blind Samson is brought to a scene of cultic revelry and taunted by his captors (16:23-25). This has now become a contest between deities: Dagon and yhwh. As weakened as he may have been, Samson stations himself in a strategic position to effect the collapse of the temple. Nothing transpires before his prayerful invocation of the Lord (16:28). But unlike former judges, he pleads not for deliverance of the people but for personal vindication. The prayer is heard and a massive destruction of the pagan enemy follows (16:29-30).

After a twenty-year judgeship, Samson was laid to rest (16:31), following a life which, if it was not always marked by virtue, was certainly expressive of faith and an abiding trust in the God of Israel.

APPENDIX

Judges 17–21

The final chapters of Judges come from the Deuteronomistic editors and are different thematically from the rest of the book. There are no judges, no vindication of Israel over pagan oppressors, no impressive leaders. In the main, they are a sad commentary on tribal life in Israel before unification. Their pro-monarchical bent emerges from a negative assessment of social life without a king and cultic life without central control. These are tales

"Samson pushed hard, and the temple fell upon the lords and all the people who were in it. Those he killed by his dying were more than those he had killed during his lifetime" (Judg 16:30).

and gave them to the silversmith, who made of them an idol overlaid with silver. So it remained in the house of Micah. ⁵The man Micah had a shrine, and he made an ephod and teraphim, and installed one of his sons, who became his priest. ⁶In those days there was no king in Israel; everyone did what was right in their own eyes.

⁷There was a young man from Bethlehem of Judah, from the clan of Judah; he was a Levite residing there. ⁸The man set out from the city, Bethlehem of Judah, to take up residence wherever he could find a place. On his journey he came into the mountain region of Ephraim as far as the house of Micah. ⁹"Where do you come from?" Micah asked him. He answered him, "I am a Levite, from Bethlehem in Judah, and I am on my way to take up residence wherever I can find a place." ¹⁰"Stay with me," Micah said to him. "Be father and priest to me, and I will give you ten silver pieces a year, a set of garments, and your living." He pressed the Levite, ¹¹and he agreed to stay with the man. The young man became like one of his own sons. ¹² Micah installed the Levite, and the young man became his priest, remaining in the house of Micah. ¹³Then Micah said, "Now I know that the LORD will prosper me, since I have the Levite as my priest."

18 **Migration of the Danites.** ¹In those days there was no king in Israel. In those days the tribe of the Danites were in search of a heritage to

---

of moral turpitude, civil war, and priestly patronage. The section is easily divided into two: the migration of Dan to the north (chs. 17–18) and the civil war against Benjamin (chs. 19–21).

17:1-13 Micah and the Levite

Micah, whose name ironically means "Who is like YHWH?" was an Ephraimite placed under a curse for stealing from his mother (17:2). Even restored, the stolen goods remained tainted, with part of the silver used to fashion an idol (17:4). His religious interests also led to his making a priestly garment (ephod) and consecrating his son a priest (17:5). His actions were reprehensible. Images, especially of YHWH, were prohibited by law (Exod 20:2-5) and priesthood, while perhaps less regulated at this early stage, was limited to Levites by the time of Judges' composition.

The locale eventually became a sanctuary for which Micah obtained the services of a Levite from Judah (17:9-10). That an Ephraimite consecrated a Levite a priest may reflect early custom when norms were less fixed (17:12; cf. Lev 8–9). Micah became the priest's patron to whom the latter was beholden (17:13).

18: 1-31 Dan

The tribe of Dan had been allocated territory in the southwest, contiguous with Judah and Benjamin. However, they never succeeded in gaining

dwell in, for up to that time no heritage had been allotted to them among the tribes of Israel.

²So the Danites sent from their clans five powerful men of Zorah and Eshtaol, to reconnoiter the land and scout it. "Go, scout the land," they were told. They went into the mountain region of Ephraim, and they spent the night there. ³While they were near the house of Micah, they recognized the voice of the young Levite, so they turned aside. They asked him, "Who brought you here? What are you doing here? What is your interest here?" ⁴"This is what Micah has done for me," he replied to them. "He has hired me and I have become his priest." ⁵They said to him, "Consult God, that we may know whether the journey we are making will lead to success." ⁶The priest said to them, "Go in peace! The journey you are making is under the eye of the LORD."

⁷So the five men went on and came to Laish. They saw the people there living securely after the manner of the Sidonians, quiet and trusting, with no lack of any natural resource. They were distant from the Sidonians and had no dealings with the Arameans. ⁸When the five returned to their kin in Zorah and Eshtaol, they were asked, "What do you have to report?" ⁹They replied, "Come, let us attack them, for we have seen the land and it is very good. Are you going to hesitate? Do not be slow to go in and take possession of the land! ¹⁰When you go you will come to a trusting people. The land stretches out in both directions, and God has indeed given it into your power—a place where no natural resource is lacking."

¹¹So six hundred of the clan of the Danites, men armed with weapons of war, set out from Zorah and Eshtaol. ¹²They marched up into Judah and encamped near Kiriath-jearim; for this reason the place is called Mahaneh-dan to this day (it lies west of Kiriath-jearim). ¹³From there they passed on into the mountain region of Ephraim and came to the house of Micah. ¹⁴Then the five

---

a foothold and so eventually migrated to the north (Josh 19:40-48; Judg 1:34). At the time of the divided kingdom, there were two major sanctuaries in the north, one at Bethel, the other at Dan (1 Kgs 12:28-30). Both were involved in illicit worship from their beginnings. The present account of the sanctuary in Dan clearly points to its unseemly origins.

Five scouts are sent from the south to reconnoiter the land, and they meet Micah and his priest (18:3-6). It may have been a different accent that makes the Levite recognizable (18:3). His credentials are tested by asking him to divine God's will, which leads to a favorable response (18:5-6).

The scouts proceed to the farthest point north, Laish, at the base of Mt. Hermon, which is the source of the Jordan river (18:7-8). They make a positive report upon returning home (18:7-10). With military force, they proceed north to make the conquest, making a stop in Judah in the region of Kiriath-jearim, gifting a part of the region with a second name, Mahaneh-dan ("the camp of Dan").

men who had gone to reconnoiter the land spoke up and said to their kindred, "Do you know that in these houses there are an ephod, teraphim, and an idol overlaid with silver? Now decide what you must do!" ¹⁵So turning in that direction, they went to the house of the young Levite at the home of Micah and greeted him. ¹⁶The six hundred Danites stationed themselves at the entrance of the gate armed with weapons of war. ¹⁷The five men who had gone to reconnoiter the land went up ¹⁸and entered the house of Micah with the priest standing there. They took the idol, the ephod, the teraphim and the metal image. When the priest said to them, "What are you doing?" ¹⁹they said to him, "Be still! Put your hand over your mouth! Come with us and be our father and priest. Is it better for you to be priest for the family of one man or to be priest for a tribe and a clan in Israel?" ²⁰The priest, agreeing, took the ephod, the teraphim, and the idol, and went along with the troops. ²¹As they turned to depart, they placed their little ones, their livestock, and their goods at the head of the column.

²²When the Danites had gone some distance from the house of Micah, Micah and the men in the houses nearby mustered and overtook them. ²³They called to the Danites, who turned and said to Micah, "What do you want that you have called this muster?" ²⁴"You have taken my god, which I made for myself, and you have gone off with my priest as well," he answered. "What is left for me? How, then, can you ask me, 'What do you want?'" ²⁵The Danites said to him, "Do not let your voice be heard near us, or aggravated men will attack you, and you will have forfeited your life and the lives of your family!" ²⁶Then the Danites went on their way, and Micah, seeing that they were too strong for him, turned back and went home.

²⁷Having taken what Micah had made and his priest, they marched against Laish, a quiet and trusting people; they put them to the sword and destroyed the city by fire. ²⁸No one came to their aid, since the city was far from Sidon and they had no dealings with the Arameans; the city was in the valley that belongs to Beth-rehob. The Danites then

Iniquity is compounded as the Danites steal sacred objects in Micah's sanctuary and prevail upon the priest to accompany them. Certain that they will be pursued by Micah and his compatriots, the Danites invert the line of march, with families and livestock going first and the military as a rear guard (18:13-21). Micah pursues but is intimidated by the superior forces (18:22-26). Reaching the peaceful and unprotected citizens of Laish, the Danites unleash a deadly force in a fiendish and brutal fashion. It is an unwarranted slaughter (18:27-31).

Dan loses no time in constructing their sanctuary and installing their priest, who is now identified as Jonathan of the line of Moses; it is his descendants who will continue in priestly ministry (18:30). Like Bethel, the Dan sanctuary lasted until the Assyrian invasion in 734 b.c. (18:30). Its life

Front view of the ancient mud brick gate of Tel Dan in northern Israel (see Judg 18:20).

rebuilt the city and occupied it. ²⁹They named it Dan after their ancestor Dan, who was born to Israel. But Laish was the name of the city formerly. ³⁰The Danites set up the idol for themselves, and Jonathan, son of Gershom, son of Moses, and his descendants were priests for the tribe of the Danites until the time the land went into captivity. ³¹They maintained the idol Micah had made as long as the house of God was in Shiloh.

19 **The Levite from Ephraim.** ¹In those days, when there was no king in Israel, there was a Levite residing in remote parts of the mountain region of Ephraim who had taken for himself a concubine from Bethlehem of Judah. ²But his concubine spurned him and left him for her father's house in Bethlehem of Judah, where she stayed for some four months. ³Her husband then set out with his servant and a pair of donkeys, and

went after her to soothe her and bring her back. He arrived at her father's house, and when the young woman's father saw him, he came out joyfully to meet him. ⁴His father-in-law, the young woman's father, urged him to stay, and so he spent three days eating and drinking and passing the night there. ⁵On the fourth day they rose early in the morning and he prepared to go. But the young woman's father said to his son-in-law, "Fortify yourself with a little food; you can go later on." ⁶So they stayed and the two men ate and drank together. Then the young woman's father said to the husband, "Why not decide to spend the night here and enjoy yourself?" ⁷The man made a move to go, but when his father-in-law pressed him he went back and spent the night there.

⁸On the fifth morning he rose early to depart, but the young woman's father

---

was co-extensive with that of the authentic sanctuary of YHWH at Shiloh (18:31), and it appears here in a very negative light. Its origins were related to stolen gods; it had enthroned idols, a subordinated priesthood, and was established in the wake of a ruthless invasion.

19:1–21:25 Civil War

There is little of redeeming value regarding tribal life in this final segment of the book; rather, the picture is one of increasing moral disintegration. It is quite possible that we are dealing with originally distinct and detached events in the story of the Levite and his concubine (19:1-14), the incident at Gibeah (19:15-29), the assembly and war against Benjamin (20:1-48), and the parallel accounts of providing women for Benjamin (21:1-14; 21:15-25). These accounts have been skillfully edited to form one continuous narrative. The pro-monarchical slant, seen especially in the events surrounding the survival of Benjamin, is much to the fore.

19:1-30 The Levite from Ephraim

Like Micah, the unnamed Levite is from Ephraimite territory (19:1; 17:1). An alternate reading for verse 2 in some manuscripts has the concubine said, "Fortify yourself!" He coaxed him, and he tarried until the afternoon, and the two of them ate. ⁹Then when the husband was ready to go with his concubine and servant, the young woman's father said to him, "See, the day is wearing on toward evening. Stay for the night. See, the day is coming to an end. Spend the night here and enjoy yourself. Early tomorrow you can start your journey home." ¹⁰The man, however, refused to stay another night; he and his concubine set out with a pair of saddled donkeys, and traveled until they came opposite Jebus, which is Jerusalem. ¹¹Since they were near Jebus with the day far gone, the servant said to his master, "Come, let us turn off to this city of the Jebusites and spend the night in it." ¹²But his master said to him, "We will not turn off to a foreigner's city, where there are no Israelites. We will go on to Gibeah. ¹³Come," he said to his servant, "let us make for some other place and spend the night in either Gibeah or Ramah." ¹⁴So they continued on their way until the sun set on them when they were opposite Gibeah of Benjamin.

¹⁵There they turned off to enter Gibeah for the night. The man went in and sat down in the town square, but no one took them inside to spend the night. ¹⁶In the evening, however, an old man came from his work in the field; he was from the mountain region of Ephraim, though he was living in Gibeah where the local people were Benjaminites. ¹⁷ When he noticed the traveler in the town square, the old man asked, "Where are you going, and where have you come from?" ¹⁸He said to him, "We are traveling from Bethlehem of Judah far up into the mountain region of Ephraim, where I am from. I have been to Bethlehem of Judah, and now I am going home; but no one has taken me into his house. ¹⁹We have straw and fodder for our donkeys, and bread and wine for myself and for your maidservant and the young man who is with your servant; there is nothing else we need." ²⁰"Rest assured," the old man said to him, "I will provide for all your

---

leaving the Levite because she was angry rather than unfaithful. At any rate, the move was unusual because the woman could not initiate divorce proceedings according to Hebrew law. The Levite's attempt at reconciliation found him and his father-in-law in remarkable accord, enjoying five days of feasting (19:4-10). The sentiments of the concubine, however, are never mentioned. On the return journey home, they bypass pagan Jebusite Jerusalem to lodge among their own in Benjaminite territory (19:10-14).

The hospitality of the man in Gibeah, who is also from Ephraim, contrasts sharply with the conduct of the townspeople (19:15-21). In fact, the repulsive gesture at Gibeah earned for it a name of poor repute. The efforts of the men to abuse the guest sexually mirrors very closely the scene at Sodom (19:22-24; cf. Gen 19:4-8), and the retaliation against Gibeah resembles that of Saul at Jabesh-gilead (1 Sam 11:7-8). In demanding the overnight guest, the men of Gibeah violated the sacred law of hospitality, but the alternative solution was equally abhorrent. By modern standards, the treatment of the

needs, but do not spend the night in the public square." ²¹So he led them to his house and mixed fodder for the donkeys. Then they washed their feet, and ate and drank.

The Outrage at Gibeah. ²²While they were enjoying themselves, the men of the city, a bunch of scoundrels, surrounded the house and beat on the door. They said to the old man who was the owner of the house, "Bring out the man who has come into your house, so that we may get intimate with him." ²³The man who was the owner of the house went out to them and said, "No, my brothers; do not be so wicked. This man has come into my house; do not commit this terrible crime. ²⁴Instead, let me bring out my virgin daughter and this man's concubine. Humiliate them, or do whatever you want; but against him do not commit such a terrible crime." ²⁵But the men would not listen to him. So the man seized his concubine and thrust her outside to them. They raped her and abused her all night until morning, and let her go as the sun was coming up. ²⁶At the approach of morning the woman came and collapsed at the entrance of the house in which her husband was, and lay there until morning. ²⁷When her husband rose in the morning and opened the door of the house to start out again on his journey, there was the woman, his concubine, collapsed at the entrance of the house with her hands on the threshold. ²⁸"Come, let us go," he said to her, but there was no answer. So the man placed her on a donkey and started out again for home.

²⁹On reaching home, he got a knife and took hold of the body of his concubine. He cut her up limb by limb into twelve pieces and sent them throughout the territory of Israel. ³⁰He instructed the men whom he sent, "Thus you shall say to all the men of Israel: 'Has such a thing ever happened from the day the Israelites came up from the land of Egypt to this day? Take note of it; form a plan and give orders.'"

20 **Assembly of Israelites.** ¹So all the Israelites came out as one, from Dan to Beer-sheba including the land of Gilead, and the assembly gathered to the Lord at Mizpah. ²The leaders of all the people, all the staff-bearers of Israel, presented themselves in the assembly of the people of God—four hundred thousand foot soldiers who carried swords. ³Meanwhile, the Benjaminites heard that the Israelites had gone up to

concubine was unconscionable. Both her husband and the Gibeahites share the guilt in her death, although it is the latter who appear reprehensible in the narrative. There is no criticism of her dismemberment, an action which was geared to create a strong reaction (19:25-30). From an editorial vantage point, the death of the concubine was seen as so serious that it resulted in an Israelite assembly.

20:1-48 War with Benjamin

As formerly noted, the war with Benjamin over the death of a single person may be more literary than historical. The picture is one of Israelites

Mizpah. The Israelites asked, "How did this evil thing happen?" ⁴and the Levite, the husband of the murdered woman, testified: "It was at Gibeah of Benjamin, which my concubine and I had entered for the night. ⁵The lords of Gibeah rose up against me and surrounded me in the house at night. I was the one they intended to kill, but they abused my concubine and she died. ⁶So I took my concubine and cut her up and sent her through every part of the territory of Israel, because of the terrible thing they had done in Israel. ⁷So now, all you Israelites, give your judgment and counsel in this matter." ⁸All the people rose as one to say, "None of us will leave for our tents or return to our homes. ⁹Now as for Gibeah, this is what we will do: We will go up against it by lot, ¹⁰taking from all the tribes of Israel ten men for every hundred, a hundred for every thousand, a thousand for every ten thousand, and procuring supplies for the soldiers who will go to exact from Gibeah of Benjamin the full measure of the terrible thing it committed in Israel."

¹¹So all the men of Israel gathered against the city, united as one. ¹²The tribes of Israel sent men throughout the tribe of Benjamin to say, "What is this evil that has occurred among you? ¹³Now give up the men, the scoundrels who are in Gibeah, that we may put them to death and thus purge the evil from Israel." But the Benjaminites refused to listen to their kindred, the Israelites. ¹⁴Instead, the Benjaminites assembled from their cities at Gibeah, to march out to battle with the Israelites. ¹⁵On that day the Benjaminites mustered from their cities twenty-six thousand swordsmen, in addition to the inhabitants of Gibeah, who mustered seven hundred picked men ¹⁶who were left-handed, every one of them able to sling a stone at a hair without missing. ¹⁷The men of Israel, without Benjamin, mustered four hundred thousand swordsmen, all of them warriors. ¹⁸They went up to Bethel and consulted God. When the Israelites asked, "Who shall go up first for us to do battle with the Benjaminites?" the LORD said: Judah first. ¹⁹The Israelites rose in the morning and encamped against Gibeah.

War with Benjamin. ²⁰The men of Israel marched out to do battle with Benjamin and drew up in battle array against them at Gibeah. ²¹The Benjaminites marched out of Gibeah that day and felled twenty-two thousand men of Israel. ²²But the army of the men of Israel took courage and again drew up for battle in the place where they had drawn up on the previous day. ²³Then the Israelites went up and wept before the LORD until evening. "Shall I again engage my brother Benjamin in battle?" they asked the LORD; and the LORD answered: At-

---

in battle array, with numbers that are undoubtedly inflated (20:2). The Levite's account of the event at Gibeah attempts to color the facts (20:4-5). He mentions an attempt on his life not heretofore indicated, and does not state that he gave his concubine to the men who abused her. The first overture made by the indignant Israelites was to ask for the extradition of the men of Gibeah guilty of the crime (20:11-13); this failing, a full-scale battle ensued

tack! ²⁴When the Israelites drew near to the Benjaminites on the second day, ²⁵Benjamin marched out of Gibeah against them again and felled eighteen thousand Israelites, all of them swordsmen. ²⁶So the entire Israelite army went up and entered Bethel, where they sat weeping before the LORD. They fasted that day until evening and presented burnt offerings and communion offerings before the LORD. ²⁷The Israelites consulted the LORD (for the ark of the covenant of the LORD was there in those days, ²⁸and Phinehas, son of Eleazar, son of Aaron, was standing in his presence in those days), and asked, "Shall I again go out to battle with my brother Benjamin, or shall I stop?" The LORD said: Attack! For tomorrow I will deliver him into your power. ²⁹So Israel set men in ambush around Gibeah.

³⁰When the Israelites went up against the Benjaminites on the third day, they drew up against Gibeah as on other occasions. ³¹When the Benjaminites marched out to meet the army, they began, as on other occasions, to strike down some of the troops along the highways, one of which goes up to Bethel and one to Gibeah in the open country; about thirty Israelites were slain. ³²The Benjaminites thought, "They are routed before us as previously." The Israelites, however, were thinking, "We will flee and draw them out from the city onto the highways." ³³And then all the men of Israel rose from their places, forming up at Baal-tamar, and the Israelites in ambush rushed from their place west of Gibeah ³⁴and advanced against Gibeah with ten thousand picked men from all Israel. The fighting was severe, but no one knew that a disaster was closing in. ³⁵The LORD defeated Benjamin before Israel; and on that day the Israelites killed twenty-five thousand one hundred men of Benjamin, all of them swordsmen.

³⁶Then the Benjaminites saw that they were defeated. The men of Israel gave ground to Benjamin, trusting in the ambush they had set at Gibeah. ³⁷Then the men in ambush, having made a sudden dash against Gibeah, marched in and put the whole city to the sword. ³⁸The arrangement the men of Israel had with the men in ambush was that they would send up a smoke signal from the city, ³⁹and the men of Israel would then wheel about in the battle. Benjamin, having begun by killing off some thirty of the men of Israel, thought, "Surely they are completely routed before us, as in the earlier fighting." ⁴⁰But when the signal, the column of smoke, began to rise up from the city, Benjamin looked back and there was the whole city going up in smoke toward heaven. ⁴¹Then when the men of Israel wheeled about, the men of Benjamin were thrown into confusion, for they realized that disaster was closing in on them. ⁴²They retreated before the men of Israel in the direction of the wilderness, but the fighting kept

(20:20-48). In the first two encounters, the Benjaminites were victorious (20:20-29), in the third, they were defeated through a clever ruse (20:30-35). The two defeats of the Israelite forces gave the impression of an inadequate military force (20:20-25). With the third attack the Benjaminites felt

pace with them, and those who had been in the city were spreading destruction in between. ⁴³They surrounded the men of Benjamin, pursued them from Nohah and drove them along to a point east of Gibeah. ⁴⁴Eighteen thousand from Benjamin fell, all of them warriors. ⁴⁵They turned and fled into the wilderness to the crag of Rimmon. The Israelites picked off five thousand men on the highways and kept pace with them as far as Gidom, where they struck down another two thousand of them. ⁴⁶The total of those from Benjamin who fell that day was twenty-five thousand swordsmen, all of them warriors. ⁴⁷Six hundred men turned and fled into the wilderness to the crag of Rimmon, where they remained for four months.

⁴⁸Then the men of Israel turned back against the Benjaminites, putting them to the sword—the inhabitants of the cities, the livestock, and all they came upon. Moreover they destroyed by fire all the cities they came upon.

21 Ensuring a Future for Benjamin. ¹The men of Israel took an oath at Mizpah: "None of us will give his daughter in marriage to anyone from Benjamin." ²So the people went to Bethel and remained there before God until evening, raising their voices in bitter weeping. ³They said, "LORD, God of Israel, why has this happened in Israel that today one tribe of Israel should be lacking?" ⁴Early the next day the people built an altar there and offered burnt offerings and communion offerings. ⁵Then the Israelites asked, "Are there any among all the tribes of Israel who did not come up to the LORD for the assembly?" For there was a solemn oath that anyone who did not go up to the LORD at Mizpah should be put to death.

⁶The Israelites were disconsolate over their brother Benjamin and said, "Today one tribe has been cut off from Israel. ⁷What can we do about wives for the survivors, since we have sworn by the LORD not to give them any of our daughters in marriage?" ⁸And when they asked, "Is there one among the tribes of Israel who did not come up to the LORD in Mizpah?" they found that none of the men of Jabesh-gilead had come to the

---

more secure and moved their troops out of the city in pursuit of the enemy (20:30-32). In abandoning Gibeah, they left their rear flank unprotected. The concealed Israelites then staged an ambush, entered and destroyed the city, putting it to the torch (20:36-42). Caught in this "pincer" strategy from the front and behind, the Benjaminite troops were in disarray and quickly defeated (20:43-47). Thus, the Gibeahites, their city, and the forces of Benjamin were decimated. This proved to be a serious insurrection and brought great damage and loss to one of Israel's tribes.

21:1-25 The future of Benjamin

Following the defeat of Benjamin, Israel was faced with a dilemma. In the heat of the assembly, the other tribes had sworn not to have their daughters marry Benjaminites. This now meant that one of the twelve tribes was faced with extinction (21:17). In determining who had not been

encampment for the assembly. [9]A roll call of the people was taken, and none of the inhabitants of Jabesh-gilead was present. [10]So the assembly sent twelve thousand warriors there with orders, "Go put the inhabitants of Jabesh-gilead to the sword. [11]This is what you are to do: Every male and every woman who has had relations with a male you shall put under the ban." [12]Finding among the inhabitants of Jabesh-gilead four hundred young virgin women, who had not had relations with a man, they brought them to the camp at Shiloh, in the land of Canaan. [13]Then the whole assembly sent word to the Benjaminites at the crag of Rimmon, offering them peace. [14]So Benjamin returned at that time, and they were given as wives the women of Jabesh-gilead who had been spared; but these proved to be not enough for them.

[15]The people had regrets about Benjamin because the LORD had made a breach among the tribes of Israel. [16]The elders of the assembly said, "What shall we do for wives for the survivors? For the women of Benjamin have been annihilated." [17]They said, "There must be heirs for the survivors of Benjamin, so that a tribe will not be wiped out from Israel. [18]Yet we cannot give them any of our daughters in marriage." For the Israelites had taken an oath, "Cursed be he who gives a wife to Benjamin!" [19]Then they thought of the yearly feast of the LORD at Shiloh, north of Bethel, east of the highway that goes up from Bethel to Shechem, and south of Lebonah. [20]And they instructed the Benjaminites, "Go and set an ambush in the vineyards. [21]When you see the women of Shiloh come out to join in the dances, come out of the vineyards and catch a wife for each of you from the women of Shiloh; then go on to the land of Benjamin. [22]When their fathers or their brothers come to complain to us, we shall say to them, 'Release them to us as a kindness, since we did not take a woman for every man in battle. Nor did you yourselves give your daughters to them, thus incurring guilt.'"

[23]The Benjaminites did this; they carried off wives for each of them from the dancers they had seized, and they went back each to his own heritage, where they rebuilt the cities and settled them. [24]At that

present at Mizpah for the vow, the name of Jabesh-gilead in Transjordan emerged (21:8). Once again the decision involved an act of terror. The city was destroyed with all its inhabitants, except for the unmarried women, four hundred in number. These were then given to the Benjaminite male population (21:1-14).

In what may well be a parallel source, now made complementary to the preceding, the number of women was not sufficient. An annual feast at Shiloh offered the opportunity for abduction, and this the Benjaminites were counseled to do (21:15-22). The proposed response to be given the girls' families was disingenuous. In accepting the fact of their abduction and generously letting things stand, the families would not be guilty of violating the vow, since the women had not been offered (21:22). Benjamin was thus assured a future, the tribe was reinstated, and peace returned (21:23-24).

time the Israelites dispersed from there for their own tribes and clans; they set out from there each to his own heritage.

²⁵In those days there was no king in Israel; everyone did what was right in their own sight.

The Deuteronomist gives his assessment of such unwarranted and unruly conduct. Without a king, people made their own choices (21:25). From his perspective, the argument has been well made, and the reader is now prepared for the rise of the monarchy.

REVIEW AIDS AND DISCUSSION TOPICS

The Book of Joshua

Introduction (pages 5–7)

1. What was Joshua's relationship to Moses? How do Joshua's exploits mirror those of Moses?

2. Joshua and Judges were written 600 years after the events depicted took place. At that time Israel was entering the Babylonian exile. How does this "hindsight" influence the interpretation of events during the time of Joshua and Judges?

3. The Israelites have a hard time keeping the first precept of the Decalogue. Find this in Exodus 20 and read it. What kind of false gods do we "worship" today? What motivates us to sometimes put other things before our God?

4. What do you think about the theme of obedience and covenant faithfulness in Joshua? Do you think it's an important one? Is it important just for the Israelites? What does it mean to us today?

5. Do you think history can ever be objective? Where do you see examples of the Deuteronomistic writer at work in Joshua? Where do you see evidence that this is a compilation rather than a narrative from a single source? What is gained or lost by this author's approach? Does it matter to you if Israel had a more difficult time conquering the Canaanites than this book suggests?

6. Most of the events in the book of Joshua take place in the region assigned to the tribe of Benjamin, although these events are meant to be representative of the entire conquest of "the land of Canaan." Look at the land given to the Benjaminites on the map. What is the significance of this place today? Why do you think it took on so much focus in this book? (This emphasis is something to keep in mind if you move on to read the history accounts in 1–2 Samuel, 1–2 Kings, and 1–2 Chronicles.)

1:1–12:24 Possession of the Land (pages 9–37)

1. Rahab the harlot makes her way into the genealogy of Jesus in Matthew 1:5. What is her role in the history of salvation?

2. How does God's appearance to Joshua as a "warrior God" in 5:13-15 compare to the burning bush appearance in Exodus 3? Compare Moses and Joshua, their missions and behavior following these appearances by God.

3. Gilgal is said to be based on etiology (i.e., cause-study, explaining why and how certain objects or customs came to be). How is the name of the place related to the story of what happened there?

4. Identify three places in the text where *herem* (the ban) comes into play. What is its importance?

5. The story of Gibeon has consequences for everyone. What is the message to the readers during the captivity? In what way is it an etiology?

13:1–21:45 Division of the Land *(pages 38–54)*

1. Why do the Levites not get their own territory? How do you understand their role?

2. Why does Caleb get territory?

3. What are the "cities of refuge" and what made them necessary? What do you think of such a system? Do we have anything comparable?

22:1–24:33 Appendix *(pages 55–63)*

1. Why was it important to the Israelites that there was only one altar, and what side of the Jordan it was on?

2. What led to the misunderstanding with the Transjordan tribes? How was it resolved? What does this incident and how it was handled tell you about the early days of Israel? Can you think of any parallels in the history of the church?

3. What sense do you have of the way things were run in the newly established lands of Israel? What might you expect the book of Judges, which tells the next segment of the history of the Israelites, to be like?

4. How does this covenant history compare with what you know of the history of Christian people with the "new covenant" established by Jesus? Consider the major themes of this book: faithfulness, obedience, ritual, and unity.

The Book of Judges

Introduction *(pages 64–66)*

1. How are these "judges" different from what we think of as judges today?

2. What does it mean that the people are led by "heroes" or "saviors" instead of by kings or magistrates?

3. Many of these stories do not square with our modern sensibilities. What do you take from them? Why might they have appealed to the audience at the time of the Babylonian captivity?

4. What do the stories of the judges tell us about disobedience, repentance, and forgiveness?

1:1–3:6 Coexistence *(pages 67–72)*

1. What infidelities are committed by the Israelites? Do they get better or worse over time?

2. What are the consequences of Israel's infidelities? How do these consequences set the stage for the stories of the judges?

3:7–16:31 The Judges *(pages 72–106)*

1. What is the nature of the heroism of Ehud? How do the stories of Othniel, Ehud, and Shamgar tell us what we need to know about who the judges are?

2. Why is Deborah's story told twice? How do the two accounts compare? What do they tell us about the composition of the Old Testament histories, and the way stories come to us? Can you think of a story you know from both a narrative and song or poem? What does your story and the story of Deborah tell us about the cultures in which they were composed?

3. How does Gideon compare to other judges? What are we learning about the ones God chooses to save Israel?

4. The troops of Gideon are reduced two times. What does this process tell us about the troops? What does it tell us about Gideon's faith and the faith of the men who ultimately go into battle?

5. What does the experience with Abimelech as king say about Israel's organization and development as a people? What might it reflect about

the author's objectives or bias? How do we look on royalty today? Do we see these governments (judges and kings) as more "primitive" than democracy? What does our attitude say about our own values and sense of hierarchy and leadership?

6. How do you assess Samson's heroism? How does he fit alongside heroes that were humble and lowly, like Abraham, Moses, and Gideon?

17:1–21:25 Appendix *(pages 106–19)*

1. What do you make of the way Dan's tribe begins its life on the land? Are they led by God or by their own counsel? What is the importance of pointing out that the sanctuary fell during the Assyrian invasion in 734 B.C.?

2. The story of Gibeah has close parallels with the story of Sodom and Gomorrah in Genesis 19:4-8. What happens in Gibeah is what the Levite feared would happen if he stayed in a Jebusite town, but it happens among his fellow Israelites. The result is civil war. In this final episode, what do you make of the way Israel works together, and the way Israel behaves first in regards to avenging the crime at Gibeah, and then in response to Benjamin's defeat? Again, are there parallels to the modern day? Are there lessons about God's mercy and justice? What other lessons can we draw from this episode?

3. Looking at the map of tribal lands and boundaries, how significant is it that the tribe of Benjamin was almost extinguished? What parallels between the current unrest in this region and the history of Joshua and Judges can you make?

INDEX OF CITATIONS FROM THE
CATECHISM OF THE CATHOLIC CHURCH

The arabic number(s) following the citation refer(s) to the paragraph number(s) in the *Catechism of the Catholic Church*. The asterisk following a paragraph number indicates that the citation has been paraphrased.

Joshua		Judges	
3:10	2112	6:11-24	332*
13:33	1539*	13	332*
		13:18	206*

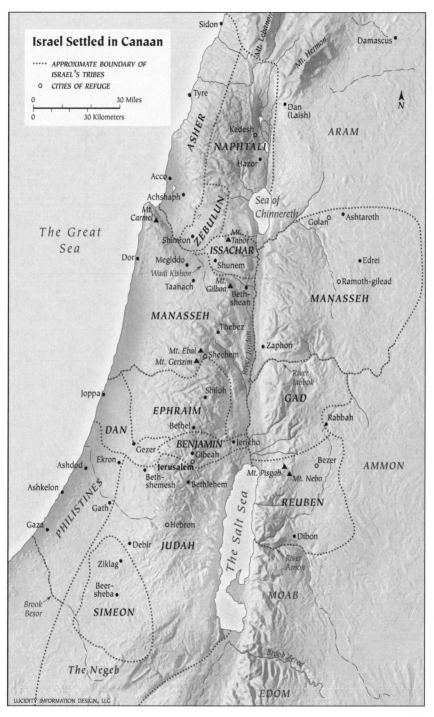

Israel Settled in Canaan

····· APPROXIMATE BOUNDARY OF
ISRAEL'S TRIBES
○ CITIES OF REFUGE

0 ———————— 30 Miles
0 ———————— 30 Kilometers

Sidon

Damascus

Mt. Lebanon

Mt. Hermon

Tyre

Dan
(Laish)

ARAM

Kedesh

ASHER

NAPHTALI

Hazor

Acco

Achshaph

Mt.
Carmel

ZEBULUN

Sea of
Chinnereth

Golan

Ashtaroth

Shimron

Mt.
Tabor

*The Great
Sea*

ISSACHAR

Edrei

Dor

Megiddo

Shunem

Wadi Kishon

Ramoth-gilead

Taanach

Mt.
Gilboa

Beth-
shean

MANASSEH

MANASSEH

Thebez

River Jordan

Zaphon

Mt. Ebal
Mt. Gerizim

Shechem

*River
Jabbok*

Shiloh

GAD

Joppa

EPHRAIM

Rabbah

Bethel

DAN

BENJAMIN

Jericho

Gezer

Gibeah

Ashdod

Ekron

Jerusalem

Bezer

AMMON

Beth-
shemesh

Bethlehem

Mt. Pisgah

Mt. Nebo

Ashkelon

PHILISTINES

Gath

REUBEN

Gaza

Hebron

Dibon

Debir

JUDAH

The Salt Sea

*River
Arnon*

Ziklag

Beer-
sheba

MOAB

*Brook
Besor*

SIMEON

The Negeb

Brook Zered

EDOM